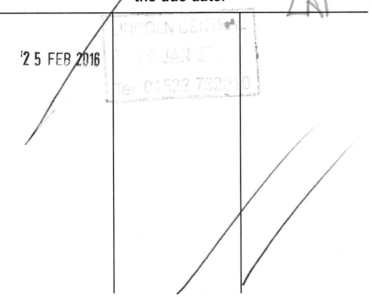

FINDING LOVE IN THE LOOKING GLASS

A Book of Counselling Case Stories

Maggie Yaxley Smith

KARNAC

First published in 2014 by
Karnac Books Ltd
118 Finchley Road, London NW3 5HT

British Library Cataloguing in Publication Data

A C.I.P. for this book is available from the British Library

ISBN 978 1 78220 124 3

Edited, designed and produced by The Studio Publishing Services Ltd
www.publishingservicesuk.co.uk
e-mail: studio@publishingservicesuk.co.uk

Printed in Great Britain

www.karnacbooks.com

CONTENTS

This book is dedicated to my husband, Chris, who has supported me on my journey.

ACKNOWLEDGEMENTS

I want to thank my husband Chris for his openness, acceptance, love and patience. It is not easy being married to a counsellor or therapist. Within our profession, there are many resources that enable and empower our self-development, our partners do not have that daily support and may often find themselves under a microscope, especially when we are training!

I want to thank all the clients, supervisees and colleagues that I have worked with for sharing their wisdom, trust and insights into how we are.

This book has been enriched by my clinical supervisor, Brian Graham, whose advice, insights and "super-vision" have been invaluable.

Thank you to family and friends who have encouraged me to write and the many writers who have inspired me with their poetry, stories, ideas and delicious words.

I want to thank the staff at Karnac for their support.

ABOUT THE AUTHOR

Maggie Yaxley Smith has worked as a humanistic counsellor, clinical supervisor, head of a university counselling service, and group facilitator for more than thirty-five years. She has worked therapeutically with a varied and multi-cultural client group on a university campus, in a women's refuge, in private practice, and for Relate. She is an accredited senior registered practitioner with the British Association for Counselling and Psychotherapy. She has an MA in Women's Studies and is a member of a well-being writing network based in Kent. She is also a Veriditas trained labyrinth facilitator.

Introduction

This is a positive book which shows how people can make different choices in their lives once they find a level of self-acceptance and realistic goals. It is a book about turning survival strategies, some of which we may be negatively attached to from early childhood, into positive choices to develop the potential of our truest selves. We are the real experts on ourselves, given the time and space to explore that all-important relationship.

There is a freedom in gradually loosening the bonds of our "adapted self" that we have learnt to develop as a way of surviving or fitting in to our families, school, culture, or society in terms of what is "expected" of us. We have remarkable abilities to learn from our mistakes and develop self-awareness. Self-awareness enables us to let go of negative attachments to the past and develop the self-esteem and self-belief that comes from a full acceptance of both our strengths and limitations. Once we can do that, we are able to develop the compassion, wisdom, and humility that enables us to experience joy, love, happiness, peace, playfulness, good health, and well-being as best we can. There is a freedom in allowing ourselves to play with life and enjoy the time we are here in a creative and interesting way.

These case stories show what can be achieved in counselling and how the counselling relationship can enable people to change their lives. All characters in these stories are entirely fictitious. The writer creates and develops the characters, drawing from her considerable experience as a counsellor, and shows how she would use her particular style of brief, humanistic counselling with them.

The counsellor

Each counsellor and psychotherapist is required to have membership of a recognised professional body and to adhere to the most up to date version of their ethical guidelines. The author is a senior accredited member of her professional organisation, the British Association for Counselling and Psychotherapy, and adheres to the BACP Ethical Framework for Good Practice in Counselling and Psychotherapy. This requires a counsellor to have regular supervision with an independent clinical supervisor, the conditions of which are specified by the relevant professional body. This supervision includes discussions of their own feelings, motives, need for support, and challenge about the work they are doing. It is an important safeguard for their clients as well as for themselves and as such it is a vital part of the professional and ethical monitoring of the counselling process. This is an opportunity for increased professional and personal development of the counsellor and discussions of such things as boundary issues and ethical dilemmas often arise in this supervision process. Each counsellor is required to have a valid professional indemnity insurance while working with clients.

The counselling structure in a typical counselling service

The assessment: each client begins their counselling with an initial half-hour assessment which may be with a different counsellor or the same counsellor with whom the client goes on to have regular counselling sessions. This initial assessment is used to confirm contact details for the clients; to answer any questions the client may have about the counselling process; to explain to the client a little about the type of counselling that will be offered; it is also used as a triage system so that each client is assessed for the severity of their presenting problem and is then placed at an appropriate place on the waiting list for regular counselling within the counselling service as a whole. The assessment is an opportunity to take a family and background history of the clients; to take an account of the presenting problem and any medical, counselling, or therapeutic history that may be relevant. There is often discussion of reading or other information that might be useful to clients having to wait some time for their regular counselling to begin. Although clients may see a different counsellor for their assessment than they see for their regular counselling sessions, all of their regular counselling sessions are normally with the same counsellor. The exceptions to this are when a client is sharing something that is particularly difficult, for example, any form of sexual abuse, suicidal thoughts, or the fact that they have found it exceedingly difficult to come and talk to a counsellor. Then, it is usual to book the client in with the same counsellor.

The counselling: the counselling referred to in this book is based on a brief, time-limited humanistic counselling model, mostly taking place over five weekly sessions. Regular counselling sessions are offered with the same counsellor, usually fifty minute sessions on a weekly basis. Sometimes, especially towards the end of the five sessions, the counselling may take place fortnightly or include one or two "check in sessions" to support specific changes that clients are making.

Appendix: at the end of this book, there is a list of useful books, articles, websites, and blogs on the topics discussed in each of the case stories.

Lan-li's story:
finding love in the looking glass

Anorexia

Recently, at a barbecue, I overheard a father saying to his petite five-year-old daughter, "don't put tomato sauce on that, you'll get fat." A shadow of hurt was cast over her previously excited face. She put the sauce bottle down on a nearby table and sat down. She chewed half-heartedly at her burger, kicking the legs of her plastic chair. I noticed that she disappeared off without finishing what was on her plate.

I never cease to be shocked by sitting across from attractive, intelligent young women or young men, listening to them tell me how stupid, ugly, and fat they are. It took me years as a counsellor to realise that such a client truly was not able to take in the truth of what was actually reflected back to them in the mirror. This distortion is just one example of the many ways we can perceive ourselves as "less than".

There are commonly two types of anorexia and although it is more frequently found in women it is something that young men can develop as well. Symptoms can begin from age ten or even earlier:

Anorexia nervosa often begins with a preoccupation with food and dieting. People eat less and less until it can become very difficult for them to eat without feeling nauseous. They lose weight and for

1

girls and women, their periods may stop completely. Some people also exercise compulsively as a way of increasing their weight loss. It can start as normal dieting which can then become compulsive or addictive and take over so that the client feels quite out of control and it becomes harder and harder to eat; they may refuse to eat with others and can develop a fear of eating in public places. Although sometimes they are knowledgeable about food and cooking and will make a point of enjoying cooking meals for other people, they may find excuses not to eat themselves. Most people with anorexia have a distorted image of their weight, size, or shape and often feel heavy even when they are very thin and obviously under-weight. They are nearly always very afraid of gaining weight. They can often be in denial of their symptoms and resist treatment until it becomes life threatening. Weight loss can escalate until it is necessary to hospitalise them in a psychiatric hospital or special dedicated unit for life saving treatment.

Anorexia bulimia often develops in later teenage years. People with bulimia eat large amounts of food in a short time. They eat quickly and although they enjoy the food at the time feel guilty or ashamed and depressed soon afterwards. They may starve themselves first and then "binge eat" or just "binge eat" but they feel as if they are out of control around food and eating. They primarily "binge eat" secretly and alone and commonly make themselves vomit afterwards. Some people with bulimia keep their weight stable but others can gradually lose weight and can get to a stage where it becomes difficult for them to eat without feeling nauseous and sometimes they may experience involuntary vomiting. Again, they can often exercise compulsively as a way of increasing their weight loss. In addition, some people may take large numbers of laxatives to purge themselves after eating or after a bout of binge eating and they may use diuretics. People with bulimia can develop excess levels of tooth decay and other gum and mouth problems from frequent vomiting.

Brief assessment summary

Client: Lan-li, British Chinese is aged twenty. She is a second year student studying for an English degree and lives in a shared student house with three female housemates who are good friends.

Presenting problem: Beginning last summer, Lan-li returned to symptoms of a previous period of anorexia bulimia in her early teens. She is now taking ten laxatives every day, binge eating, and making herself vomit two or three times per week. She has lost about twelve kilograms of weight in the last few months and is down to just under forty-five kilograms. She is five foot six inches tall. She agreed to cut down on laxatives over next week or two.

Family background:

Mother: British Chinese, born in London to parents who left China in 1955. Father: American Chinese, now British citizen. His parents emigrated to USA in early 1950s and live in New York City. Brother: Nico is fifteen. Close to maternal G/M (grandmother) who died when Lan-li was thirteen. Maternal G/F (grandfather) died when she was sixteen.

No religious affiliations.

Heterosexual but no boyfriends.

Hospitalised in psychiatric hospital special unit for bulimia at fifteen on and off for six months. Overall eighteen months of individual therapy followed by group therapy and family therapy with mum and dad. No recurrence until last summer.

Referral from: GP in her university medical centre.

First session of counselling

Lan-li Gan is shown into my room. I shake her small cold hand and invite her to sit in the comfortable chair opposite me. She sits down, neatly folded in the centre of her chair, hardly touching the surrounding arms. Her child's size jeans are sealed tightly onto her long skeletal legs that disappear into a loose fitting black jumper. Her black hair cascades over her shoulders accentuating the fact that her head seems too large for her body. Her features remind me of a Chinese brush painting made with fine but firm lines. She has wide cheek bones and perfectly positioned dark brown eyes adorned with long lashes. She is beautiful but her skin is pale and she does not look well. She shifts her gaze from her knees to make eye contact.

> Counsellor: I'm sorry you've had a bit of a wait since your assessment. I've got the notes from that meeting that you had with Janine. As you know we'll be working together for five sessions so how can I help you?

She lifts her hand to place her hair behind her ears, then she folds both of her hands on her lap beginning to move a silver filigree band on the middle finger of her right hand. She is intent on this movement back and forth as time moves slowly. She looks at me again and I notice her shallow breathing and sweat gathering on her upper lip. I smile at her. I know how difficult it can be to begin.

> *Lan-li:* I . . . em . . . my doctor told me to come and see someone. She thinks I need help.
>
> C: And what about you, do you think you need help?
>
> L: Well . . . I don't seem to be coping.

The silence grows and she looks away as tears well up, fill her eyes, flow down her cheeks, and drop into her lap. She wipes away her tears with small movements of her hands and looks around. I gently indicate the box of tissues set on a small table right beside her. She takes a tissue and wipes her eyes.

> L: I'm sorry, I told myself I wouldn't cry.
>
> C: It's okay with me, there's plenty of room for tears here. Do you want to start by talking about how you're feeling?

She wipes the tears away and the tissue gets smaller and smaller in her hand.

> L: I feel . . . I feel ashamed. I mean I know what I'm doing is stupid. I thought I'd put this behind me years ago. I can't believe I've allowed myself to go back to those old habits of making myself sick. I know how destructive it is. I can't believe I can be so stupid. It's just that . . . I look in the mirror and all I can see is this fat, ugly, stupid person. I don't seem to be able to get anything right. Even if I try and eat normally now I feel sick.

She rocks forward and hugs herself. I feel as if I want to hug her too. She looks lost and vulnerable. She takes another tissue, blows her nose, and looks out of the window. Her tears slow and she makes eye contact with me.

> L: I'm sick of being me.
>
> C: I'm interested that you put it like that in the light of your bulimia.
>
> L: Yeah . . . maybe I'm just expressing how fed up I am with myself.
>
> C: Well, I notice that you've just made three comments about yourself using the word "stupid".

L: Have I?

She looks surprised.

C: Are you always so hard on yourself?

L: I guess I've been pretty hard on myself this year. There just seems to be so much to do and I know I'm not working effectively. I'm disappointed in myself and I'm tired . . . really tired.

There is something in her eyes that draws you past her beauty and intelligence into a deep pain.

C: Well, it's frustrating when we think we've beaten something and we find ourselves getting back into old patterns of behaviour and you're going to feel tired if you're making yourself sick. I see from your notes that you've been feeling like this since the summer. What do you think the trigger might have been for you beginning to make yourself sick again?

L: Well . . . I was going away on holiday and hated that I looked really fat in a bikini.

Lan-li re-arranges her top so that it covers more of her and folds her arms in front of her flat stomach.

C: I notice that you seem to want to cover your stomach.

L: I'm afraid of you seeing how fat I am.

C: Are you aware that this is a misperception, that you are in fact considerably underweight, even though I'm sure your experience of being fat feels very real?

L: Somewhere I know it is but as you say I still see myself as really fat and that you'll think I'm ugly.

C: Do you think if I told you what I really thought about the way you look that you'd be able to hear what I said?

Lan-li and I both smile at each other and it is a shared knowing.

L: No, I guess I wouldn't.

C: Was there anything else that happened during the summer that might have been a trigger?

Lan-li's jaw tightens and she puts one of her hands over her mouth. Her breathing becomes shallow and she looks down at the floor as she talks to me.

L: I had a big row with my mum. She was going on at me about how disappointed she and my dad were that I hadn't got better marks in my exams last year. She was hassling me about doing more work in the summer before coming back to Uni. this year. She doesn't get that the first year exams don't count and it's more important to make friends. I admit I didn't work as hard as I could have but I'm more focused this year and even last year I still got an overall 2.1.

C: That sounds pretty good to me. Were you able to explain that to your mum?

L: There's no point really, she doesn't listen. I just feel that whatever I do is never good enough for her ... I know everything about me is a disappointment to her.

C: How does that feel for you?

L: Sometimes it makes me feel like giving up ... numbing out ... maybe that's when I binge eat. Food fills an emptiness that seems literally to gnaw away at my insides ... the food comforts me until I then feel bloated and just as uncomfortable being too full. Then I feel as if there's no choice, I have to make myself sick ... even with food, I don't feel I can get it *right*.

C: Have you talked to your mum about how you feel?

L: Not really.

Lan-li looks out of the window and it feels as if she has gone away. This happens as she talks about her mother and feelings.

C: It sounds like you want to do well on the course?

L: Yeah, it's interesting and no-one else has complained about my work. I've got some great housemates and they're interested in working as well as having a good time. We don't just mess around.

Lan-li sounds quite defensive, as if she is justifying herself to her mother.

C: In the assessment notes, it says that you were diagnosed with bulimia when you were fifteen.

L: Yeah, I started by taking more and more laxatives and then I found I could easily make myself sick. I lost a lot of weight and felt good about myself. I felt ... in control ... strong. I've missed that feeling.

C: How long did that last?

L: About eighteen months. Initially, mum was actually pleased that I lost weight but eventually even she got worried. During that time I spent six months in and out of hospital.

C: Did that include psychotherapy?

L: I saw someone for a few months and then joined a group for about a year, which was cool. It helped me to understand what was happening and it was good not to feel a freak. I read quite a bit about bulimia on the web and stuff but I still felt helpless. I got too weak to go out with my friends and felt more and more isolated . . . I knew I could have died . . . that *it* was in control of me instead of me being in control. I think part of me didn't want to help myself. I didn't want to come back from that place.

C: So what helped you to get through it?

L: This will sound weird. But when I really didn't care if I died or not, I felt the presence of Por-por, my grandmother. It was a kind of dream but not a dream. She died when I was thirteen and she'd been this tiny person but had great strength in her arms and I felt her pulling me up. This happened several times.

C: What was it about your grandmother that helped you?

L: She had a strong presence especially when she was silent. I knew she loved me no matter what I did. I felt protected by her . . .

Lan-li looks far away . . .

L: The scent of jasmine reminds me of her and her house. I felt at home there. I stayed with her often, more than Nico, but we both stayed with her when mum and dad were away on business trips together . . . I knew she didn't always agree with things mum said to me but she'd never criticise her to me . . . She'd just soften the blow. She had her own ways. She could be strict but there were hugs too. She didn't mind if we made a mess and . . . she always had time for us . . . she was really cool. She'd tell me stories about people she'd known when she was a child. She brought our Chinese culture, the language, and especially the food and festivals alive for me . . . She had a way of making ordinary things funny. Some of her stories would be in a mixture of Cantonese and English and some of the words she'd use were just made up but we always understood what she meant. I'm sure it was my love of her stories which encouraged me to read so much and study English. Mum was very like my grandfather who was always busy with work. Por-por was a link to our past whereas mum wanted to put her past behind her.

She struggles with tears but by tightening her chin and jaw, she stops herself from crying. She covers her mouth with her hand.

L: I didn't realise that I still feel her loss so badly, it actually hurts in my throat.

C: It sounds as if she's been an important person to you and still is. Your face lights up when you talk about her.

L: Yeah?

C: Can you tell me a bit more about your family background.

L: Well, Por-por and my grandfather escaped from China in the early 1950s on one of the last boats to leave. They'd both been from rich and powerful families and had to leave many of their family and friends behind including their elderly parents, who refused to leave and were eventually killed. Some family members went into hiding or made it to Hong Kong and came to the West later. They'd been seen as enemies of the state. The person she felt worst about was her sister, who hadn't been well enough to travel with them. She died weeks after they left. Por-por didn't talk about her feelings so much but I knew they'd been really close. Sometimes she would just sit in silence and we knew not to disturb her. She had a cousin who would visit and they would sit in silence together, sometimes for hours at a time. Afterwards, she would say that they had been visiting home. Por-por used to tell me that her soul had split into two and half had never left China.

C: It must have been very hard for them to leave.

L: My grandfather had carefully planned their escape and managed to smuggle out precious stones, enough to make a new life in London. They had two friends and some family there who helped them. My grandfather worked very hard to re-build a successful family business, trading in silk. My mum was born in London and despite them wanting a large family, she'd been their only child. Dad was born and grew up in New York City where his parents had settled in the early 1950's. When he visited London as a young man he met and fell in love with my mum. Once they married, he never returned home to live in the States again. He and my mum both worked in the business and took it over completely when my grandfather died. They've been very successful too.

C: Is there pressure on you to work in the family business?

L: I couldn't bear the thought of working in the business. I'd be bored to death.

C: And you have one brother?

L: Yeah, Nico is fifteen. He was born just after I started school.

C: How do you get on with him?

L: I'm reasonably close to him now but when I was a teenager, after Por-por died, I sometimes had to spend more time with him than I wanted to. I'd get angry with him when he'd mess me around. I resented the fact that he was a boy and he seemed to get away with anything. He was accepted for being who he was with no pressure about what he wore or what he looked like. I was jealous of his freedom. I guess now though there's more pressure on him to study business and go into the family company.

C: How would you describe your relationship with your mum and dad?

L: When I was younger I used to be much closer to dad. Mum and I had a difficult relationship. She's always been critical of me and sometimes I used to think that she was jealous of me and dad. He and I shared a love of American Football and the *Giants* in particular. We used to watch the NFL [National Football League] on TV together. Occasionally, if dad had a business meeting in New York and the *Giants* were playing at home, his dad would get us tickets. Dad would even persuade my mum to let me fly over and watch a game with them. We'd stay with his family.

C: It sounds as if you and he shared something special. Was Nico interested too?

L: No he's totally into Arsenal along with all his school mates. It's something dad and I share along with his family in New York. Mum doesn't particularly get on with dad's family. It's okay but she's just as happy if he visits on his own.

C: Tell me a bit more about you and your mum.

L: Well . . . as I said before I'm not the daughter my mum would have liked. We used to constantly battle over clothes. I was too much of a tomboy and lived in jeans and T-shirts. She would get on to dad about it a lot. She was always buying me fashionable dresses . . . the kind of thing she would wear. She wanted to show me off to her friends. I hated it. She was always on at me to lose weight.

C: Do you think that contributed to your bulimia when you were fifteen?

L: I'd kinda got used to her criticism. I felt the pressure to be "perfect" like her. I think what was worse for me around that time was when my father got really angry with me for binge eating.

Lan-li is agitated. She chews and picks at her nails.

C: What happened?

L: He found me in the kitchen late one night eating chocolate ice cream straight from the carton. He then saw loads of empty bags of crisps and peanuts and assumed it was all me. He slapped my face really hard and told me I was greedy and that I was making myself fat and ugly. I had a bruise and small cut on my cheek the next day where his ring had been. The thing was, I'd had a friend round for the evening and it had been both of us, but I wasn't about to tell him that. I was very hurt and angry with him.

Lan-li looks distressed and continues to attack her nails.

C: You still seem distressed about this.

L: I'm sorry . . . I talked about all this in the therapy then but I still get upset. I was devastated that he hit me. I honestly believed that I must be a terrible person to have made him do that. He'd shouted before but he'd never hit me. He apologised, telling me that he'd been very stressed at work, but something felt broken between us. I felt as if I'd become unlovable . . . that even my dad had stopped loving me. In the hospital I had a few sessions with my parents and we kinda sorted it out but it took me ages to trust that my dad could still love me. We'd always been so close when I was younger and I felt that something had ended between us with me growing up. I stopped going with him to New York until last year . . . Mum was surprisingly good . . . for once, she really seemed to understand. Her relationship with her dad had been very important to her and one of the reasons why she'd worked so hard in the business. She told me she'd felt connected to him through the company even after he'd died. She and I shared something at last. We began to talk a bit more and even do more things together.

C: Did that help you to recover?

L: I think it helped to be able to talk things through with my mum and dad. I knew my dad was upset about what had happened. They were both worried and felt guilty and I hated myself for doing that to them. That isn't what I wanted. I hadn't really thought about how it was for other people. I was amazed that what I did could affect other people. Even Nico had been upset by what I was doing. I felt guilty then and I decided I had to stop what I was doing for them all . . . even for Por-por . . . just knowing that she would've been so upset. Also, I was bored with obsessing about food and exercise. I was sick of weighing myself constantly. I felt as if I was living in a box. But it wasn't easy. It was hard to eat without feeling nauseous all the time. And I was scared . . . really scared of getting fat again.

As she talks about her recovery she looks brighter.

C: It sounds as if you have all the information you need about bulimia itself and that you worked really hard to recover before. I believe that you'll get back on track much faster this time because of that. My experience is that many of us have things we learn to do when we're young that seem like good survival strategies at the time; even when what we do is actually harmful. You need to remember that you've been able to move out of this behaviour before and perhaps we can look together at what might help you now. It's common to get back into old behaviours when we're feeling particularly stressed. What do you think you're left with from last summer? What might have been particularly stressful for you?

Lan-li takes time to really think about it.

L: I'd thought that everything was okay in my first year but mum worrying about me doing well enough made me doubt myself again. I realised that I'd messed up last year, as usual, and really doubted whether I could get through this year. Although I was panicking about getting fat and wearing my bikini on holiday, I think I knew this was a distraction.

C: I'm not sure that you "messed up last year". Are you a bit of a perfectionist?

Lan-li laughs.

L: My mum would laugh to hear you ask me that.

C: Why do you think your mum would laugh?

L: Because compared to her, I'm a mess. She keeps all her clothes perfectly wrapped in their original wrappings. Her office is immaculate. She always looks perfect even first thing in the morning. She's successful in everything she does.

C: That sounds like a lot to live up to, but your mum's had lots of practice to be good at what she does and you're a different person.

L: I suppose she seems so sure of *who* she is, what she's doing with her life and I've no idea what I want to do.

C: Lots of students have no idea what they want to do after university. Have you visited the Careers Service?

L: No, I've haven't.

C: Well, maybe it's a good time to get some information and advice on what's available out there.

L: I'm not even sure if I'll get through this year without messing up.

C: Well, it sounds to me as if you actually did very well last year in making friends, getting used to university life, finding good people to live with this year as well as actually getting good marks. So maybe it's a bit like you seeing yourself as fat. It seems to me there's a gap between how you really are and how you perceive yourself.

L: Do you really think so?

C: What's important is what you think.

L: I can see what you mean. I do focus on what I get wrong.

C: Is that because anything less than perfect won't do?

L: Yeah . . . I get very down when I get work back. I always think I could have done better. I got an essay back from last term which I'd been told I got a seventy-three for and when I got it back, I'd only got seventy-one. I was devastated.

C: And yet that is still a first class mark.

L: Maybe I'm more like my mum than I thought.

C: With very high expectations?

L: Yeah, all the way through school. I thought I was stupid if I didn't get the highest possible mark.

C: So this is something we can work on together in the coming weeks. You noticing just how well you are doing and thinking about what would be "good enough" for you.

L: I can see that there were high expectations from my family. I know mum felt she had to do well as she was an only child. She went straight into the business at eighteen. She told me that she only relaxed and made some friends once my father started working in the company. He was good for her. It sounded as if she had more fun once they'd got together. I know when my grandfather died work took over for both of them.

C: Did your father have high expectations of himself too?

L: He's more laid back but I think he found it harder once they were left with the company. He felt the weight of responsibility. He works all hours and I suppose he's quite driven.

C: Okay, so you've told me quite a lot about your family. Now, let's find out more about *Lan-li*.

She smiles a little shyly.

L: What do you want to know?

C: Tell me a bit about what you like to do. What makes you feel good?

L: Well you already know I like watching American Football . . . It's fun chilling out with friends . . . watching DVD's in the house when every-one's in . . . I like dancing in the nightclubs in town when I have a bit more energy . . . I hate it though when anyone gets drunk and leary . . . I suppose most of all I love reading . . . I get so involved in the different worlds created in books. I hate coming to the end of a good book . . . I used to write poems but I don't have time to do that anymore.

C: Did you enjoy doing that?

L: Yes but I'd get frustrated because they were never good enough.

C: Well that's a surprise.

We both laugh.

C: What kind of things did you like to write about?

L: Films . . . people . . . beautiful places would inspire me to want to say more, go deeper.

C: Okay, I have a suggestion for some homework. No pressure though. Sometimes it's helpful for people to do something in between the sessions, to continue with your own process.

L: Okay.

C: What I suggest is that you have a go at writing a poem about yourself, about this process, about anything we've talked about . . . whatever appeals to you to write about. What do you think?

L: Not sure what I'd write but I'll give it a go.

C: I want to emphasise Lan-li that I don't have any expectation of you doing this in a certain way. It's important that you don't feel that you have to write something *perfect* for me. You don't have to make it *right* for me . . . just allow whatever comes to you to be what it is. It's entirely up to you if you want to share it with me next time or not.

L: Okay, that feels easier.

C: Good. As we're coming to the end of the session, I'd also like to suggest that you spend some time this coming week noticing how you talk to yourself. The most enduring relationship that we ever have is the one with ourselves. We're with ourselves night and day from the moment we're born until the day we die. It's helpful for us to become aware of what beliefs we hold about ourselves; how we think about; feel about; care about; and talk to ourselves and especially how you feel in your body. As with any relationship in our lives, anything we can do to improve that relationship is beneficial. It's easier to improve something once we realise what is already going on in the here and now. What do you think?

L: I didn't realise until you mentioned it at the beginning how many times I said the word "stupid" about myself. Is that the kind of thing you mean?

C: Exactly, gradually we can wear ourselves down if we are too negative about ourselves, just like any other relationship. I'm reasonably sure that people wouldn't stay friends with us for very long if we kept calling them "stupid".

Lan-li nods.

L: I get what you mean . . . I've never really thought about having a relationship with myself . . . If we think about ourselves too much . . . wouldn't that make us selfish or self-obsessed?

C: I believe that if we can create a good relationship with ourselves by becoming more honest and accepting about both our strengths and our limitations, that self-awareness helps us to free ourselves to have better relationships with other people, even our work, in all kinds of positive ways.

L: It sounds kinda obvious when you say it like that.

C: That doesn't make it an easy thing to do. Don't worry about changing anything this week, just notice how you are with yourself. That's an important first step in making any change.

L: Okay.

I reach for my diary.

C: Let's find a time for next week.

We make another appointment for the following week and I show Lan-li to the door where we shake hands. Her eyes look brighter and she has more colour in her cheeks. I watch her walk away for a few moments and think about the world she's brought into the room with her. None of us stand alone. Each family has its own history, culture, set of beliefs, patterns of behaviour, skills and talents, some positive and some harder to deal with. I jot down a few extra notes about key issues, family history, and the homework I had suggested to her. I think she will get back on track pretty fast. She has gained a lot of awareness about what is going on for her from her past experiences and she is very bright. I really like her.

Second session of counselling

I walk down to the waiting room and there is Lan-li sitting in a corner of the room. She looks up and smiles. We greet each other and walk down the hallway to my room chatting a bit about how very cold it is. I notice she is clutching a brown envelope. In my room she takes off her dark grey coat, hangs it on the coat stand, and sits down fairly close to the edge of her seat. She looks a little more comfortable than the previous week and immediately makes eye contact. She smoothes out the brown envelope sitting on her lap.

C: So, how're you doing?

L: I wrote something, it's probably really bad, but I brought it along anyway.

C: Is really bad another way of saying "stupid"?

We both laugh.

L: I've been noticing that I do put myself down quite a lot. I think maybe I do it before other people have time to get in a negative comment. There's another girl, Emma, in my house and she's even worse than me. We're helping each other to notice how we talk to ourselves which is making it more fun.

C: That's great.

She hands me the envelope and I open it. There is one sheet with a poem on it.

C: Would you like to read it out?

L: No, I couldn't . . . but you can read it.

C: Is it okay if I read it out loud?

L: I'd rather you read it to yourself.

C: Is it okay if I read it now?

She nods and I read it to myself. Lan-li begins to pick at her nails.

> *Echoes*
>
> A granite tapestry reaches into the sky
> touching clouds that passed by long ago
> in another unknown land.
> It casts long shadows into our hearts and minds.
>
> Shadows red with flowing blood and liquid guilt
> permeating all survivors.
> No amount of washing with hard work
> can wipe us clean. There is no path
>
> home. So cobbling together strands of
> belonging, we weave something new,
> with echoes of the past silky soft
> as the skin on my grandmother's cheeks.

C: This is powerful Lan-li. I love the image of a granite tapestry and particularly the last line.

L: I realised after we talked last time that my grandparents, my mother, and me . . . we're linked by the past . . . a bloody past with family killed because they were elderly or sick but also because they happen to be born with money . . . The guilt of leaving family behind and the guilt of being a survivor. There was a sense of being damned if you were strong and damned if you weren't.

C: Do you believe that?

L: In a way . . . I was good at school and some people disliked me for it but also the better I did the more was expected of me . . . I never felt I could be good enough and I still don't. Also, I don't know if I'll ever feel that I really belong anywhere. It was hard for my mum and her parents who had no home to go back to. For my dad and his family, it was a choice to leave their country for something better. It's much easier for me but I'll always feel "different" here. I don't know what it's like to feel that ease of belonging to a country and culture that some of my friends take for granted. I've had to work harder at fitting in.

C: I'm sure you have . . . how do you feel about working with me being a white, British counsellor?

L: It feels okay and I feel you have a lot of experience of my problem.

C: Could you tell me if it got in the way of us working together?

L: I think so. I've no experience of living in a place where most people are Chinese. When I go to see my grandparents in New York, they live on the edge of Chinatown, it's a bit like that there and it feels kind of weird.

C: In a good way?

L: Yes and no . . . it can be quite threatening, especially as I haven't spoken Cantonese very much since Por-por died. Mum and dad speak mainly English together. Some of my childish language is in Cantonese but my grown up language is English.

C: I remember a conversation with a Swedish friend about living in different cultures. She'd moved to Germany and tried so hard to be German in everything she did, the way she ran her home, learning the language, cooking German food, the way she organised her work, etc. She found it exhausting and it seemed that whatever she did ended up being wrong and people there would tell her that. Then she moved again, first to America and then to England. She'd become wiser and more confident about doing things her own way wherever she was.

L: I like that. I think I try too hard to please other people.

C: I want you to know that you don't have to please me.

L: It helped me to write the poem that you told me that before . . . I still wanted you to like it but I was doing it more for myself, even a little for Por-por . . . I know she accepted me no matter what I did.

C: I appreciate you sharing it and I would encourage you to play with words more . . . I can see you have an energy for writing. Can I keep this copy?

L: Of course, if you want to.

C: I do. I like it and I want to take time to read it again later. If you choose to do any others and you want to share them here, I'd be happy to read them but I don't want that to inhibit you in any way.

L: Okay, I'll see how I feel.

C: So, how would you like to use today?

L: I felt good after last week . . . I've been surprised by how much I do talk to myself in my head and I am critical . . . nagging myself constantly about the smallest details . . . I feel guilty about not being good enough . . . and I'm anxious to get things right.

C: Did you notice how that affects you in your body?

L: I feel tense in my stomach and especially in my shoulders, and my breathing speeds up as soon as anything is expected of me, especially by myself . . . sometimes it's almost like gasping for breath, my hearts thumps really hard and I get panicky . . . quite a lot.

C: Do you feel like that here, now?

Lan-li moves herself back into her seat, taking up a bit more space.

L: I felt like that while you were reading my poem but I've calmed down.

C: What were you anxious about?

L: I thought you'd laugh or say how stupid it was.

C: That must be hard for you, carrying around that expectation of being hurt.

L: I guess it is.

Lan-li tries to smile defensively but I can see tears well up in her eyes.

C: I'm sorry that you feel like that.

She weeps quietly for a minute and then takes a tissue from the box beside her, wipes her eyes, and blows her nose.

L: I guess it's always there . . . inside . . . the waiting to be found out . . . found wanting.

C: So it would seem important that you have someone strongly on your side . . . like yourself . . . caring for yourself.

L: Well, I've realised that taking laxatives isn't very caring.

C: How have you got on in cutting down on them since you had the assessment?

L: I was able to cut down to nine a day . . . I got scared about taking any less in case they didn't work at all . . . wasn't sure if I'd be able to go to the loo without them . . . but it was okay.

C: How many do you take now?

L: This last week I've cut down to eight a day.

C: It's good if you've cut down. Could you maybe continue to take a few less each week and see how you feel.

L: I know it's stupid but I'm so scared of not taking them.

C: It's that word again . . . it's not stupid to be afraid of making changes. Do you think that you could cut down by two more this week . . . As you've said, it's an important part of you taking care of yourself. This relationship with yourself is what will eventually support you in all the changes you make.

L: Okay, I'll try.

C: Mmmmm, I often query that word "try". My experience is that it can be a way of saying "I don't really want to do that." It's a bit like the difference between saying: "I want to do something" and "I will do something"; one shows more commitment than the other. What do you think?

L: I see what you mean . . . Okay, I'll cut down to six for one week.

C: Great, you sound more positive.

L: Also, I didn't make myself sick this past week, although I went running a bit more to make up for it.

C: How did that feel?

L: I think the running made me feel better. I ate more sensibly even though I still feel nauseous when I eat. I even went out for a pizza with Emma and Becky . . . I haven't been as focused on food . . . It felt good to write something and I had an essay to prepare for.

C: It sounds as if you're getting back on track.

L: It felt good to tell Emma that I was coming here and share with her some of what I was doing, especially the idea of us having a relationship with ourselves. When I've felt bad, I've mostly pretended to other people that everything is "fine".

C: That was brave of you to talk to Emma. What do you think some of your other strengths are?

Lan-li puts her hand over her mouth as if to stop herself speaking out and she looks down.

L: Emm . . . that's difficult . . . I think I work reasonably hard at my course. I'm quite organised, mostly. My desk is a tip, but I kinda know where everything is . . . I mostly keep in touch with home and friends, through Facebook and e-mail . . . I'm quite careful with money.

C: I notice that you qualify your strengths, with "quite", "mostly", and "reasonably". What do you like about yourself?

L: Emm . . . I do my share in the house . . . I'm quite reliable.

C: Quite?

We both laugh.

L: This really is difficult isn't it?

C: Perhaps you're more used to reflecting on your limitations.

L: Yeah, that's much easier . . . I suppose I care about my friends and housemates . . . that's about it.

C: I notice that you haven't mentioned anything that you like about your body.

Lan-li gives me a knowing grimace.

L: That's a hard one for me. I hate the way I look.

C: What about the way your body works and moves?

L: I'm quite a good dancer. Oh no . . . friends say I'm a good dancer.

C: Do you say, you're a good dancer?

L: Ohhh . . . yes, I suppose so.

Lan-li smiles and shakes her head but she takes her hand away from her mouth.

C: Do you have photographs of yourself as a child that you like?

L: Not really . . . I was an ugly child.

C: Perhaps if you began with appreciating the small child within you, it would be a place to start raising your self-esteem. Would you like to do a short exercise on that?

L: Depends what it is.

C: Well, I'm going to ask you to think about what age you might have first experienced yourself as "ugly". Then I want you to imagine that small child in the room, sitting on your lap, and imagine beginning to build a relationship with that child. Do you want to have a go?

L: Okay, I'm up for it.

I get up, pick up a small turquoise silk cushion from an empty chair against the wall near the door and sit back down holding it on my lap while I explain more about the exercise. Lan-li stays sitting back in her chair but is still chewing the side of one of fingernails.

> C: Okay, first of all I want you to think of an age when you might have felt most vulnerable and unacceptable in some way, perhaps you or someone else using the word, "ugly".

Lan-li loosely hugs her stomach and leans forward as she is thinking about this.

> L: Around six . . . I remember being friends with a boy in my class called Oliver who I'd been at playschool with and suddenly he stopped wanting to play with me and told me I was ugly. I was very unhappy at school for a while . . . there were a few racist comments from one or two of the boys once I didn't have the protection of Oliver. He didn't join in . . . I think he felt badly about it but he didn't stop them either. Eventually, I made friends with a girl called Alice. We're still in touch occasionally.

> C: Did you talk to your parents or teachers about what was going on?

> L: No . . . I felt ashamed . . . I wanted to disappear. Alice and some of the other girls stuck up for me and gradually I became one of a group of girls who were quite sporty. I missed playing with the boys though and especially Oliver. I didn't see him out of school any more either.

> C: Have you come across other racist comments?

> L: Not really, I think once I found a group of friends, it was okay. Bullies seem to sniff out people on their own or anyone "different".

> C: I'm sure you're right. Do you still feel that vulnerability sometimes?

> L: I feel vulnerable when I'm in a new situation . . . I fade into the background in a group of people sometimes.

> C: Shall we begin this exercise?

> L: Yeah.

> C: I'd like you to put this cushion on your lap, shut your eyes, and imagine that this is six-year-old year old Lan-li sitting on your lap.

I pass the turquoise silk cushion over to Lan-li carefully. She places it on her lap and gently holds the sides of it. She shuts her eyes.

> C: What would she be wearing?

> L: She'd be wearing jeans and a navy T-shirt with trainers and navy socks.

C: How would she wear her hair?

L: She'd have it straight down to just above her shoulders with a shiny blue slide holding back her hair to one side.

C: I want you to close your eyes now and imagine the cushion on your lap being little Lan-li.

She shuts her eyes tightly and gently hugs the cushion up against her tummy.

C: What would you most want to say to little Lan-li?

L: That she's not ugly. That Oliver wanted to play with the boys and didn't know how else to tell her.

C: So tell her.

She hugs the cushion and talks very softly to the imagined little Lan-li:

L: You weren't ugly . . . Oliver didn't mean what he said . . . He wanted to play with the boys and felt bad about that as you'd been good friends . . . He wanted to push you away . . . He felt bad and made you feel bad. You don't have to feel like that anymore.

C: I want you to imagine the place inside you that is the source of your love. Imagine that large pool of love and then I'd like you to imagine that little Lan-li, exactly as she is, is able to shrink to a small enough size to fit into that pool of love inside you. I'd like you to take a few moments to imagine what it feels like for her to be immersed in that pool of love inside you . . . then I'd like you to allow yourself to feel what it's like for you to keep her safe inside that pool of love . . . This is where she needs to live now. Imagine what that might feel like for both of you . . . take as much time as you need before coming back into this room.

Lan-li tightly hugs the cushion to her. Her eyes are closed but moist with unshed tears. There is a warm silence in the room . . . She eventually opens her eyes and smiles through watery eyes.

C: I'd like you to notice a colour and shape in this room to ground yourself back in this place.

Lan-li looks soft faced and a little dreamy as she takes a few moments to look around the room.

C: How did you experience that?

L: Mmm . . . it felt very real and moving . . . I was a bit self-conscious at first. I wanted to do it right. Then little Lan-li was just here and I wanted to take that hurt and confusion away from her. I felt like she was a part of me that I can like and look after. She seemed so little and it was weird, nice weird but weird . . . I'm tired but kinda relaxed tired.

I offer to take the cushion and place it gently back on the seat it came from.

C: It's getting close to the end of today's session. Anything else you'd like to say before we end?

L: No, I feel as if I want to take myself off for a walk round campus and be with myself and that's unusual for me.

C: Good, I hope you do. Do continue to notice how you talk to yourself this coming week and how your body is feeling as well. Also, if you have any photographs of yourself and want to bring them along, do. It's great that you've decided to cut down on the laxatives, I wish you luck with that.

We make an appointment for the following week and Lan-li still has that soft smile on her face as she walks off down the hallway. That exercise is one that several people have found valuable as a way of re-connecting themselves to their inner child.

Third session of counselling

I had an urgent phone call with a GP about another client so I am running ten minutes late when I go to collect Lan-li. She is walking up and down the hallway rather than sitting in the waiting room. I apologise for cutting her time short. She is carrying a brown envelope in her hand and she is wearing a bright green jumper over her jeans. There is a real sparkle about her. Lan-li sits down and looks more comfortable in her chair. Her hair is tied back with a bright green band revealing more of her face.

C: You look lovely with your hair back.

L: Thank you. Emma, Becky, and I have been playing with different styles.

C: How do you want to use today?

L: Well, I brought another poem. This one was a surprise for me that just came out when I sat down to write some notes up.

C: That's interesting. Would you be willing to read it out to me?

L: Not ready for that yet but I don't mind if you read it out.

C: I'd be glad to.

Lan-li smoothes out the brown envelope and passes it to me like a precious package. I open it and read it out loud.

> *The Imposter*
>
> You look at me intently,
> your eyes screwed up with criticism.
> I can see the image cut deep into your retina
> of what should be.
> Your longing for her makes my heart ache
> with the emptiness of a gap
> that I can't fill and can't be.
> I will always be second best.
> That shiny fantasy
> that steals your love away from me.
> I can only be this flesh and blood imposter,
> alive and real and here.

C: Where did that come from?

L: Well, as well as noticing what I've said to myself, I've begun to challenge some of the things that I find myself thinking and feeling about myself. That exercise last week was important for me to see that there is that little part of me that needs feeding with approval not criticism. I thought about how critical my mum has been and I realise that I've never felt I could be good enough for her. Then I took over being critical of myself.

Lan-li looks pained and grabs a tissue as her eyes fill with tears and she bites hard into her lips. She wipes her eyes and blows her nose.

L: She's not like that now . . . but I wasn't the way she wanted me to be . . . the way she'd imagined I'd be. I wasn't like her. I didn't like fashionable clothes, strappy sandals, silver and gold bangles, sparkly earrings, frilly, lacy, stylish dresses, silk scarves, designer handbags, and well cut hair.

C: Maybe it's helpful for you to consider what kind of woman that you are and what kind of woman you want to be. Part of being at university, and this particular stage of life, is about that transition from adolescence to adulthood. It can be very much about finding our own identity both in relationship to ourselves and in relationship to the world. Think about what people, and in particular what women, you admire in real life, in books, and in films.

L: I've never thought about who I want to be . . . don't think I ever thought I had a choice. It's always been, "be like mum, be successful, and be right or don't be like her, be a failure, and be wrong" . . . I think I even worked hard to be different and I can see that even when I was reacting to her, I probably wasn't me either. I've been quite tied to mum haven't I?

C: Well our parents are strong role models for us but we have other role models too.

L: I think I know who I don't want to be but not what I want.

C: There's still time you know.

L: Yeah . . . perhaps I'm in too much of a hurry. And I've got to get it right haven't I?

We both laugh.

C: You can just take one step at a time.

L: Yes, but in which direction?

C: Maybe it's okay not to have all the answers sometimes. Perhaps you need to be able to tolerate not knowing for a while.

L: Oooh that sounds scary.

C: Well let's look at the direction you've taken by coming here. Part of what I heard you say about your recovery at fifteen and sixteen was that it became important for you to recover for other people in your family. Maybe, this time, now you're twenty, it's important for you to choose to recover for yourself.

L: I do want to get better . . . it's unfamiliar for me to want to do anything good for myself but I don't want to feel trapped in this old behaviour and way of thinking forever.

C: Well the fact that you're here and want to change this means that you're more than half way there . . . and really working at this. How did it feel for you to hear me read out your poem?

L: I was still tense, but I liked hearing my words set free, out into the room. What did you think of it?

C: I think you write well. The bit about feeling second best was sad but I enjoyed the ending in which you were strong and assertive. You seem more confident about your writing too.

L: I was excited about sharing it with you. I do love playing with words and finding my voice.

C: Well, I guess that is all about finding you too. A life's work I think!

L: I do feel I'm doing the right degree for me, so maybe I need to see how I feel when I finish it, take one step at a time.

C: That sounds good. Some of it is being able to trust that you will make the right choices for yourself.

L: I think it's hard to move from doing what pleases others to trusting that I can even know what choices are good for me.

C: Have you experienced your choice to come here for counselling as a good choice?

L: I really have . . . also I can't believe that I've been able to share my poems . . . my words . . . my deepest feelings with you . . . it's been like walking into a dark tunnel and finding a light at the end . . . and that can be scary too.

C: Yes, trust is about risking . . . risking success as well as failure.

L: Well coming to Uni. is a great place to test that out.

C: How did you get on this week with cutting down on the laxatives?

L: "I cut down by half, to four laxatives and yesterday I cut down to two. I was afraid that I wouldn't be able to go to the loo at all but I could. After that work last week on my six-year-old, it felt wrong to take them. I know it's harming me and I don't want to do that anymore . . . I haven't made myself sick either because I haven't binged. I've felt more in balance this week around food but I do feel nauseous when I eat . . . doing exercises helps to relieve some of the huge tension I feel about the danger of getting fat again.

C: That's really encouraging for you to have cut down to only two. I'm really pleased for you.

Lan-li smiles broadly.

L: I'm pleased too . . . and something else . . . I went home at the weekend and I brought back some family photographs.

Lan-li bends down to retrieve a turquoise A4 folder from her bag, takes off the elastic closer and takes out one framed photograph of her grandmother and a small pile of loose mixed size photographs. I clear space on the nearby coffee table and suggest she lays them out there. I position the table so we can both see them. The first one she selects is the framed photo which she carefully stands up on the table. She then lays out the other photos of her and her family in order of age, the first ones baby photographs and the last ones of her from when she was a young teenager. There are about fifteeen of them. I lift up the framed photograph to get a closer look.

C: Your grandmother is beautiful and I can see that you take after her.

L: Do you think so . . . This is my favourite photograph of her.

I set it back down on the table.

C: So when you look at these photographs, why do you think you chose these in particular and what do they tell you about yourself and your family?

L: Well, the picture of Por-por I keep on my bedside cupboard. I know it's silly but I talk to her all the time.

C: That's understandable and not at all *silly*.

Lan-li grins at me when I emphasise the word "silly".

L: I haven't been doing so much of that this week . . . well . . . I think these pictures were most representative of my family. What I notice is . . .

She points out several photographs of her as a baby and small child.

L: . . . these photos are taken by mum so she isn't in them and I'm being held by Por-por. My dad's only in these two but he's in more when I'm older and wearing more normal clothes. These photos of me in dresses which are so extravagant and voluminous are hideous even this one in the pram and look at these horrible layered party dresses as a four-, five-, and six-year-old; I hated them. I remember there was one school friend's birthday party when I was soooo overdressed and some of the girls were really mean. I didn't want to feel different. I look so fat in those dresses . . . and I can see . . . when I'm wearing normal clothes that I wasn't actually fat . . .

C: Did that surprise you?

L: I can see, looking at these, that I felt uncomfortable in the clothes mum made me wear. I felt awkward, and big, and yes, fat. You can see when I began to dress in jeans and T-shirts, I started to feel much more comfortable and I'm smiling more . . . not in this posed one of the whole family which was the only one I could find with my grandfather in . . . I notice here that Nico wasn't stuffed into old fashioned baby clothes, he was free to move around.

C: Has it been useful to look at these?

L: It has. I can see some of what has made me feel uncomfortable about my body. I don't blame mum 'cos I know she wanted the very best for me. I really get her even though it's driven me nuts over the years. I think she used to feel she had to do everything perfectly, including being a mum. She's much more laid back now . . . Looking closely at these photos has helped me to understand that feeling uncomfortable in my clothes as a baby and small child may have got confused with feeling uncomfortable in my body and I need to find some peace with myself and my body.

C: Anything that helps us understand our past and the source of negative patterns can help us to change. Looking at old photos can be helpful.

C: I'm aware that we haven't really talked about your feelings about your body in terms of your sexuality. I noticed that on your assessment form you said you hadn't had any long term relationships.

Lan-li immediately hugs her stomach with both arms and leans forward, a protective move?

L: Yeah, I've liked a few guys, one of them, Will, the brother of one of my housemates, Suzie . . . but I guess I back off when I like someone. I kinda reject them before they reject me.

C: You talk about backing off, are you aware of what you did with your body when I raised this?

L: Wow, I wasn't but I am now . . . I guess it is something I need to talk about.

C: So, can you say something about how you feel just before you *back off*?

L: I feel shy . . . nervous . . . exposed. I don't really know what is expected . . . so it's easier to run away.

C: What do you think might happen if you didn't run away?

L: They might think I'm interested in them and if they aren't interested in me, I'd feel humiliated . . . I'm afraid of looking stupid. Then what if they're interested in me and I'm not interested in them . . . I'm a bit afraid of the whole thing of relationships, sex, how to say no . . . let alone how to say yes. I'm afraid of getting it *wrong* and it seems as if there is so much at stake so it's so much easier to choose to avoid that whole thing.

C: I'm sorry that as we began late it's already time for us to end now so it seems as if it might be useful to talk about this some more next time.

L: Scary but yeah. I'd like to be less scared of men. Maybe there's a part of me not really wanting to grow up. Well, I've risked writing—twice; showing you photos; now sex . . . I might be the one who's late next week.

We both laugh and Lan-li stops hugging her stomach and sits back in her seat.

C: What I would suggest, is that you specifically notice how you are this week around men that you like or are attracted to. Notice your body language and what messages you might be giving them and how you feel in your body.

L: Emm . . . okay.

C: We've got two more sessions left. How does that feel for you?

L: Okay . . . it's gone very quickly and I'd love to have another ten sessions but I accept that time is limited and it's up to me to make the changes. It's like you said the first session, having recovered before, it's easier to get back on track . . . I'm not sure I believed you then.

C: You've worked hard in between sessions and been willing to take risks so I'd like to suggest some more homework that might be helpful. We talked about choices earlier and I wonder if you could notice how you make choices, any choices . . . which way you walk across campus; what music you play; how long you wait once you recognise that you want to go to the loo; what you choose to do for fun; what you choose to eat: for example, whether you want something hot or cold, sweet or savoury; where you choose to eat . . . all those small choices that we make every day. Just becoming more aware of how you choose and what your process is can help you know a bit more about yourself. Do you choose for yourself or do what pleases other people? What do you think?

L: Yeah, I don't think I've ever thought about it. I know I find making decisions difficult. I'll think about it.

C: It may be that if you felt more confident about deserving to make the right choices for yourself and felt more confident in your ability to assert yourself, relationships with men wouldn't be so frightening either.

Lan-li looks very thoughtful as we make an appointment for the following week but as she leaves I notice that she somehow takes up much more space in the room.

Fourth session of counselling

Lan-li is walking up and down the hallway and seems both excited and a bit anxious to begin. She is again wearing her hair back off her face and she is wearing a pretty blue patterned shirt and even some mascara and lipstick. I compliment her as she comes into the room and she is a little shy about it.

> L: No poem this week but I have been thinking about guys. I asked Emma to help me to notice what I do around them. I realise that I hold back in conversations. I look down a lot, thinking that if I can't see them, they can't see me. Emma told me that I avoid dancing with men . . . I love dancing but I only dance with girlfriends and stop if any guy is looking like they might ask me to dance with them. I get very tense when we go to a club and there's someone there I like and sometimes I even hide in the loo to escape.

> C: What do you think you're afraid of?

> L: I just don't want the hassle. I see how some of my friends get into problems sexually; maybe getting deeper into relationships before they're ready and I don't want that. There is such an expectation.

> C: I understand what you are saying, maybe we can come back to this and first look at what came up for you in thinking about how you make choices because maybe these two issues are linked.

> L: Yeah, I see what you mean. Well . . . I did notice that often I just go along with what's easy at the time. I realised a silly thing . . .

I gently shake my head

> L: . . okay not a silly thing . . . I've swopped the word silly for stupid haven't I?

> C: Maybe that's just the beginning of changing it altogether.

> L: I hope so. This week, I realised that sometimes I would hold on when I wanted to go to the loo because I didn't want to excuse myself and leave if someone was talking to me . . . Then, I remembered that I missed a seminar a few weeks ago because a friend was talking to me about her boyfriend who she thought was cheating on her. We'd been talking for ages and it was an important seminar for me on a topic I want to do an essay on later this term. I got notes from a friend but I needed to go and chose not to because I didn't want to leave Jessica . . . I'll often ask for a drink that I know is easy, that someone else is having too and the same

thing with food. I can see that it's the little things that are actually important. I ignore what I want . . . I find it almost impossible to say no to someone and I can hold a door open for ages if there is someone coming through after me, to a ridiculous degree.

C: I understand that it's hard to say no but would you really want someone to do something for you because they may be afraid to say no?

L: No way, no way . . . I'd feel terrible.

C: But, that's what you're doing to other people.

L: Yeah, I see that.

C: It's important for you to realise that you have a choice and you could still decide to stay with a friend because they are in need and miss a seminar or not, but you need to be conscious about that process of making the choice. You were saying in the previous session that sometimes you didn't feel you had a choice, but you do.

L: Yeah, I get that . . . I do have a choice . . . and that it's okay, no, more than okay, it's important to say no if that's what I really want to do . . . otherwise it's not fair to anyone . . . I've never thought of it like that.

C: It's important to realise that when we make a choice, it's both a freedom and a responsibility.

L: It really is.

C: You know I've sometimes suggested to people I've worked with, who have a similar pattern of wanting to please, that they focus, even just for a day, on not leaving the door open for people behind them. It can show us how afraid we are of upsetting other people and can enable us to become a little more tolerant of not always feeling you *have* to do it . . . so it becomes a choice of something we do because we want to . . . and it may take less time to get around campus!

Lan-li looks at me wide eyed and anxiously twisted her ring around her finger.

L: I'd find that impossible.

C: Well, thats quite a strong reaction . . . why do you think that might be impossible?

L: I guess I'm seriously afraid of upsetting people . . . not being liked . . . not being accepted . . . even just the thought of letting the door go on someone makes my stomach feel tight . . . like I do when I've done something wrong. It goes back to being "different" . . . I'm afraid people make less allowances for me because I'm Chinese . . . there's a certain pressure that has lived inside me all my life.

C: Has it been your experience that people have made less allowances for you?

L: I don't know . . . I suppose it's a bit like always feeling a polite guest rather than being in your own home, kicking off your shoes, and slobbing around . . . I think I've picked up that feeling from my mum . . . as if she'd brought me into someone else's house and I needed to behave particularly well. I don't feel like that with my friends . . . I did with one or two very "English" teachers . . . sometimes there might be something I didn't understand which was "cultural".

C: That would be understandable. Are you aware of that pressure now?

L: I feel it when I'm home but not here at Uni . . . the great thing about being here on campus is the number of students and staff from all over the place . . . there's a freedom here to be myself . . . but there's a pressure to behave well . . . It feels bad to imagine not opening the door for someone and I can stand for ages holding the door open for people. It would be a freedom to feel that I don't *have* to. I'd still do it for an elderly person and I think that is because I do respect old people more than my English friends, partly because of Por-por but also that is a part of my culture that I feel good about.

C: So perhaps it's important to acknowledge the richness of some of those "differences" which you want to choose to keep.

L: I know that I'm proud of being Chinese and English.

C: So we come back to choices again. You can choose to not open the door to people and see how it feels if you think that would be useful for you.

L: I'll think about that.

C: If we come back again to relationships, perhaps you can choose to be freer in those too. You can choose to take relationships more slowly.

L: As I said last week, I guess part of me doesn't really believe anyone will be interested in going out with me and rather than be let down, I back off, so I can't be rejected.

C: It's a risk. If you back off then you can be sure that there is no risk of you going out with anyone, but is that what you want?

L: No. I haven't really let myself know what I want but I know that I do want to have someone special in my life to share things with.

C: How did you experience your parent's relationship? After all, they're your role model of how relationships work; your grandparents too.

L: Well, mum and dad were often not around because they worked very hard in the business and still do but I've seen them have fun together and with friends, trips abroad, and stuff. My dad looks at my mum sometimes and I know he thinks she's beautiful, I can see it. He is more affectionate. She holds back more but I've heard them laughing together at private jokes. She gets angry with him quickly but calms down quickly. He's a bit afraid of her and will placate her or go quiet. He'll shout at Nico and me and then he's fine with us but he hardly ever shows his anger to her. Por-por and my grandfather didn't show their physical affection. They were often silent with each other but it was a silence that was full and respectful. He could be severe with all of us and a little frightening. He had a fierce look and would be quick to anger. Por-por would laugh at him, especially if he was being pompous, but it was with a light touch. My dad's parents are always bickering and he gets embarrassed by them but it's just who they are. I think that's why he's more inclined to go quiet.

C: Did your parents ever talk to you about sex.

L: No, never . . . Por-por told me about it all after I told her a joke that I heard at school. She wasn't at all embarrassed. She stopped what she was doing, made some tea, and sat me down. She made it sound important as she explained about the differences in a man and a woman, feelings, bodies, periods, love-making. She was lovely and made it all sound rather romantic as well as matter of fact. I felt as if I had stepped onto a path of womanhood and it felt special. It made sense of all the bits of information I'd gathered at school in jokes and things. The way Por-por told me made it special; a secret knowledge. She wasn't shy about things like that. After that, when I heard jokes I would tell her and she'd laugh a little behind her hand and then tell me not to repeat it to anyone. Mum assumed I'd done it at school. I know my dad spoke to Nico in a "man to man way" 'cos Nico told me that he'd felt really awkward. He and I had talked about it all ages before when he did it at school."

C: How lovely your grandmother sounds.

L: You'll set me off and I was determined not to cry this session.

We both smile.

C: It sounds as if you grew up with a positive view about relationships.

L: Except that one with myself.

C: So what will enable you to risk changing your behaviour around young men you like?

Lan-li again hugs her stomach and leans forward.

L: That feels hard, my whole stomach is turning. I guess I need to learn to flirt a bit—that's what Emma says I need to do.

C: What do you think you need to do?

L: Well, I think she's right but I've no idea how to be like that.

C: So watch people over the next week or so, see how they are with each other, notice who you want to flirt with a bit, or just be more open to them. You can make friends with someone first and let it develop slowly. It can be however you want it to be. After all, you have a choice about all of it.

L: Oh you make it all sound so easy but it isn't. How will I know if someone likes me?

C: Well if you're looking away, you won't be able to see whether anyone is interested in you but if you continue to notice how someone is looking at you, you will certainly have more information and it seems to me that you need that information about young men around you. How do you know when you want to be friends with people?

L: I listen to them. I notice what we have in common. Maybe I like their energy. I join in conversations and share what I think and feel more. I might agree to do things with them or even suggest doing things with them. Emmm . . . I don't do that with guys. Oh, I feel like I'm starting this when I'm too old. It feels too difficult.

Lan-li looks agitated and is busy twisting the ring on her finger round and round.

C: Take it easy, find your own pace, and notice how people communicate interest to each other and to you. Notice your own body language. Think about how much you've discovered in the last few weeks just by becoming more self-aware. Remember, one step at a time. Maybe you need to take more risks, starting with small ones.

L: Okay. I'll begin by not looking away all the time and not running off to the loo. I need to stay with the discomfort, like I've done with *not* making myself sick and *not* taking the laxatives.

C: Exactly . . . How did you do with that this week?

L: Well, you won't believe me, but I didn't take any pills this week, or be sick, or anything. I exercised in an okay way; not overdoing it.

C: I'm so pleased for you. You've really persevered and succeeded. It just shows how committed you are to getting well. Well done.

L: I keep thinking I'm going to mess up but it's all going okay. I like this feeling. I'm still taking it a day at a time.

C: I wonder, as next time will be our last session, if you want to have a few weeks gap to really feel confident about being on track before we meet for that last session. What do you think?

L: That feels scary but since coming here I'm getting used to being scared.

We both laugh out loud.

C: Good!

L: If everything falls apart, can I come back before then?

C: If you need to, you can ring me and we'll talk on the phone first.

L: Okay.

C: If we arrange to meet in three weeks for our final session, it gives you time to put some of these things into practice so you can feel self-assured about the changes you're making. I don't think you will need to come back after that, but of course, if something else happens or you want a top up session at any point, again, you can ring me and we can decide that together. When you first came, you were highly motivated and you've proved that by using the counselling extremely well.

L: You've made it easy for me to talk and I do feel more confident. My course is going well and I thought about what you said about other role models. As this was a reading week I took some time to read Jung Chang's *White Swans* and *The Bone Setter's Daughter* by Amy Tan. It's weird that I've never read anything written by Chinese woman before.

C: How was that for you?

L: It helped me to connect with stories Por-por told me. I saw how lucky I am to have such rich roots. I understand mum more and see why she put pressure on herself and me to be perfect.

C: In what way?

L: She and my dad have thrown themselves into the business world. Most of their friends are from that world and some of those relationships are social rather than intimate. It's been very important for them to be socially as well as financially successful; to get things right. Their closer relationships are with various cousins and other family, perhaps with different pressures, but that's where they relax. They are an in-between generation here determined to prove themselves and be British.

C: What about you?

L: In some ways it's easier for me. You know why? I can choose . . . I can choose to own the best bits about being Chinese and even the smaller part that is American yet despite everything I've felt before, this is my home. I had a glimpse of it last summer during the Olympics. It was so good to be in London and feel part of something international but more than anything I was proud of being British. I was proud of being part of a multi-cultural country with people from all over chatting and even hugging each other in the street when someone else got a gold medal. Despite what was going on for me then, it was an exciting time. I have been afraid of being "different" but that feeling of being part of something much bigger than me has come back.

C: It was a special time.

L: It really was.

C: When it comes to choosing what kind of woman you want to be, I have a rather practical suggestion of something to do in the next few weeks, especially relevant to the photographs you shared last time. I thought it might be useful for you to visit some of the many charity shops around and try on clothes that you would never normally wear, all sorts. The idea is to play with this, take a friend or do it on your own, but the idea is to test out seeing yourself in many different styles, textures, and colours of clothes. Find out what you feel most suits you. Discover what type of clothes you enjoy wearing and what compliments your body. It may help you build a more positive relationship with your body. Not all clothes suit everyone and some of it is having more information about what enhances your own shape and colouring. It may mean letting go of an expectation of looking like a stretched photograph or a size zero model. It is about experimenting so that you can find out what helps you to look and feel the best you can, as yourself. What do you think?

L: I hate buying clothes and the whole process of having to see myself in mirrors so I usually just take something from the racks and try in on at home. You find the things for me to do that are most scary.

C: I know this is a challenge for you. Are you willing to do it?

L: Yeah. I can see that it is again about choosing what I like and realising that some things look bad on me and some things look okay and that everyone is "different" in that way. I don't spend time looking at my body. The mirror has always been my enemy.

C: Who do you think is looking in the mirror?

L: Well, I guess it's me . . . I get that I'm my own enemy.

C: What do you tell yourself about your body?

L: I look at everything that is wrong . . . that isn't *perfect*.

C: It sounds as if you have a bully sitting on your shoulder whispering into your ear.

Lan-li's eyes well up with tears and she twists her ring round and round.

L: . . . I feel quite sick when you say that . . . I know that's true and I want to be free of that voice because it's exhausting . . . how do I make it go away?

C: Do you know where it comes from?

L: "Films, television, magazines . . . I notice all the girls who are really slim and *perfect* . . . my mum's voice comparing me to other people, not so much now but she used to . . . my fantasy of what is *expected* of a woman to be successful.

C: It sounds a very heavy load to be carrying through your life. What a shame not to be able to see how lovely you are right now.

Lan-li looks at me directly.

L: Do you really mean that?

C: Of course I do but can you believe what I'm saying?

L: I don't know . . . I want to.

C: So much of this is about beliefs and we can choose what we believe . . . to see the glass half full or half empty.

L: I'm afraid of believing that I'm okay . . . what if I relax too much and become fat?

C: It's hard to trust yourself if you are used to forcing yourself into a position. It's a risk . . . to trust yourself . . . to trust that you're okay . . . that you will be okay . . . that you can look after yourself in a good way and get it wrong sometimes but still make it okay. There's a freedom in believing in yourself and an element of surrender . . . maybe that's the risk.

L: Yeah, it's a risk . . . I can choose to see the glass . . . me . . . as half full rather than half empty. The pressure of living up to some fantasy of perfection is too much . . . it builds up inside me until I get so scared and tense. It has made me ill.

C: Yes it has.

L: Well, I've learnt that I can get it wrong and come back from that. That makes me feel like I can relax a bit about who I am and what I do. Seeing the glass as half full enables me to focus more on today . . . this week . . . what I want to do with my life. When I do that I feel good about myself.

C: Do you see the large number 70% stuck on my noticeboard?

L: Yeah.

C: Well I read somewhere that if we exercise our muscles, 70% is giving them a good work out and stretching them just enough. If we do more than 70%, we move towards putting a strain on our muscles. It is just there to remind me to remind people I work with that 70% is stretching ourselves and challenging ourselves to a high level in many different areas but for so many of us there is an expectation of perfection, 100%. Perhaps if we lower those expectations of perfection, we can choose to be happy instead.

L: That reminds me of that essay I got back and the actual mark was 2% less. I can't believe how upset I was that it was 71% instead of 73%. What a waste of feeling bad when I could have been really happy about it.

C: We all do it. Think how some people feel who get a silver, or bronze medal, or come last.

L: Yet they've done well to get to the Olympics at all. Wow, I can see what I've done to myself by believing that my body is too fat. I'm so lucky to have escaped from all this with being healthy. I could have really destroyed my body.

C: Well, I have another one of my suggestions, a pleasant one this time. In these next few weeks before we meet again, why don't you buy yourself a present, to celebrate your choice to recover. What do you think?

L: Emmm . . . I like that idea. I've no idea what to get but there's time to think about it.

C: So shall we make an appointment in three weeks?

We make an appointment and Lan-li asks me for a hug on the way out. I give her a hug and it feels like an ending of the actual counselling. The next appointment will be more of a check-in session to see how she is doing.

Fifth and final session of counselling

Lan-li is sitting in the waiting room wrapped up in a beautiful royal blue jacket. Her eyes are shining and she has cut her hair to just below her chin and it is well shaped to frame her face. She looks older; more her age. She looks womanly. As we walk down to my room I told her how fantastic she looks and for the first time, I feel she accepts and takes in the compliment. She hangs up her jacket and underneath is wearing a light pair of very feminine fitted trousers and a slightly low cut and "fitted" teal coloured shirt which shows off her figure.

C: So its three weeks since we met and you look amazing.

L: I've put on some weight but for the first time I'm saying that as a positive thing . . . I feel okay. I still feel tense when eating but there have been times that I've forgotten about food and weight and have just been getting on with my life . . . I stayed off the laxatives for two weeks and then started taking them again for a few days when I was invited to a party with some old friends in London. I nearly made myself sick the day before the party and in that battle with myself, I suddenly realised that I would rather not go to the party at all than harm myself. Just knowing that I had that choice made me realise how ridiculous it all was to make approval from other people more important than my health, my own body . . . It was an "aha" moment for me and I ended up throwing away all the laxatives that I'd stashed away. I went to the party and totally enjoyed myself dancing and chatting to friends I hadn't seen for ages. Since then, I've been busy finishing my essays for this term and have even begun to do a bit of revision.

C: Do you know which individuals you were actually seeking approval from?

L: When I think about it now, it wasn't anyone else. It was me.

C: That's important to know and you did well to get yourself back on track. I hope you are very proud of yourself.

L: I am . . . and there's more . . . I've even written a couple of poems and have sent them off to the English Department's poetry competition; haven't heard anything yet.

C: That's suitably risky.

L: I'm finding that it makes me more anxious to hide away, not less. Taking risks is becoming a habit . . . not too much of a habit.

We both laugh and I notice how much Lan-li seems at ease with herself. She has put on weight but in all the right places and she has colour in her cheeks. She looks healthy.

L: After last time, I did go with Emma to try on clothes and I went on my own a couple of times. I don't often do things on my own. It was fun and I bought a few things that I would never normally wear; this top and a bright turquoise dress; which I wore to the party. I've only owned one proper dress, bought for the First Year Ball, which has since been shoved to the back of my wardrobe. I discovered that I like clothes that are more feminine, I still like wearing trousers most of all but I've even painted my toe nails.

She slips her feet out of her shoes, no pumps this time, and her toes are painted a lovely bright red.

C: They look fantastic.

L: I know . . . I can't paint my fingernails because I still bite them so I thought I would paint my toenails. I've even begun to flirt a tiny bit or at least not always look away from men as much. I haven't met anyone I like yet but I have noticed a bit of interest. I'm still scared but I feel as if I'm walking around the swimming pool dressed in my new swim suit ready to jump in; or rather walk in the shallow end.

C: I love that metaphor and what a great place for you to be, taking it all at your own pace.

L: Another thing . . . I went to Paris with mum. She was going on business and rather than go with dad, she asked if I wanted to go along and make it a long weekend. We had a lovely time walking up and down the Seine and round the shops. We even went to the market in Saint Dennis, which she wouldn't normally go to and which I loved. She bought me this jacket and some high suede boots which were totally different for me. I should have worn them . . . The day she was busy working I spent on my own enjoying the Musee D'Orsay and fell in love with a polar bear there in the main hall. I sat down right beside it and wrote a poem, which was one of the poems I've sent off. Also, there is a sculptor, Charles Cordier who had made sculptures of Oriental and African figures which I found inspiring, so much art in London and Paris is white European. I read a bit about Van Gogh, that he was inspired by Japanese art that he collected and I saw his paintings differently and enjoyed them more ... We found an antique shop with lots of Chinese art and figurines and we were tempted to buy one of them but they were too expensive in the end. It was fun though. It was good to find some objects and art that connected me with my roots and to share that with my mum ... I'm talking non-stop ... sorry.

C: It is lovely to hear you so excited and you really fill up this room with your energy.

L: It really helped to spend time with my mum. I told her a bit about how I felt ... well, before we went to Paris, I shared that poem with her, *The Imposter*. I felt bad because it made her cry but we really talked for ages and she apologised. She told me that she felt she had had to be like a boy. She knew that her father had been disappointed that she was a girl. He was disappointed that I was a girl too. Anyway, because she felt forced to be like a son, she wanted me to feel good about being a girl which is why she put me in fancy dresses. Isn't it weird how we all carry different stuff from our childhoods. She was being caring of me by wanting me to feel good about being a girl and all the time I was more of a tomboy. Maybe, I too picked up those messages from my grandfather at a young age that being a girl was second rate and then I ended up feeling second rate because I wasn't the girly girl I thought my mum wanted me to be ... wow, life is complicated.

C: That's why I love the title of the book, *Families and How to Survive Them*, by Robin Skinner ... Sometimes, we can unpick aspects of the past and redesign, or rather "re-decide" ourselves, if we understand where it begins. Often it doesn't begin just with our immediate family but from the generations before that. It's powerful to become aware of the source of the patterns that take us away from being our true selves. We can then choose to find the way back home to ourselves. I think children are amazing in the way they find strategies to survive and cope with whatever comes at them in early childhood. The great thing is to learn that we can choose to change those strategies when they don't fit us so well in adulthood. It feels as if you've done just that ... not only in these sessions but since you began to think through some of these things for yourself at fifteen. We learn far more from the things that go wrong for us than from the things that go right.

L: There was I believing that I had to strive for perfection.

C: When it's a life long journey instead to strive to be ourselves.

We look at each other and there is a real sharing of what it is to be human. Sometimes I feel that Lan-li is wise beyond her years and perhaps that is the influence of her grandmother that she carries with her.

L: I know it's gonna take me a long time to accept my body, if I ever do, but I've decided that I want to be healthy. I don't want to damage my body any more. It will take time for me to achieve a healthy weight without being afraid. I'm a bit scared of becoming a grown up. When I was a little girl, life seemed less complicated . . . I do have more idea now of the kind of woman I want to grow into.

C: Do you know how you'd like your life to be in say, two years' time?

L: I think, if I can get good marks, I'd like to go on and do a Masters . . . wow, I haven't allowed myself to say that before . . . I enjoy studying and putting together pieces of work and maybe I'd like to do a Creative Writing MA . . . that would leave me options to teach, to write, to get into journalism, research, or something like that . . . I'd like to be comfortable around food and not feel anxious when I go out for a meal or cook. I'd like to learn to cook Chinese food. There's a pile of Por-por's recipes at home, in Chinese, and no-one uses them. I could translate them. I want to improve my Chinese . . . also I'd like to go to China . . . Mum and I talked about it when we were in Paris . . . maybe we could go as a family and visit the various regions where my grandparents were born and grew up . . . maybe one day I could write *their* story.

C: What a fantastic idea.

L: Yeah . . . Also, I'd like to have a boyfriend . . . I'd like to have stopped biting my nails so I need to be much less anxious . . . can't think of anything else.

C: Well, that's quite a lot . . . What do you already find helps you to feel less anxious?

L: Going to the gym uses up some of that excess adrenaline . . . not drinking too much coffee . . . if I sit and listen to music that is soothing but I find it hard to stop and do nothing.

C: Would it be useful for me to run you through one short and one longer relaxation that you could do on your own?

L: It would. I keep meaning to download a meditation but I never get around to it. It would be good to have something I could do when I know I'm going to eat out or going to a party 'cos that's when I get agitated.

C: Well, one of these is very short, a few minutes, and the other one is longer and more of a visualisation. So, make yourself comfortable in your chair and if you want to take your shoes off, please do. It's good if you keep your feet flat on the floor so you can feel grounded and when you're ready close your eyes and take a few deep breaths . . . Breathe in easily and imagine the air passing through the top and middle of your lungs and being drawn deep into your abdomen, just above your navel. Just a few deep breaths . . . and then allow your breathing to return to an easy normal breath. As you do this, imagine you are being held by your chair, really held and supported. Feel that sensation of being held and supported and just gently focus on your inhale and your exhale. Don't force them, just notice your breathing in and your breathing out and if any thoughts come in to your mind, just let them come in and drift off again while you focus on your inhale and your exhale. We're going to do this for just a couple of minutes and during that time, I just want you to continue to imagine being held and supported by your chair and keep noticing your breathing in and your breathing out . . . and when you're ready, open your eyes and notice a colour and shape in the room to ground you back here.

Lan-li slowly opens her eyes and looks around the room, her breathing has slowed down and she smiles.

L: That was cool and although it was short I felt as if it calmed me.

C: That's a short one you can do almost anywhere and if it's a busy place, you could even do it in the loo. Are you up for doing a slightly longer one?

L: Yeah.

C: It would be good to begin in the same way, making yourself comfortable in the chair, feet flat on the ground, and eyes shut. Feel yourself being supported and held by the chair and draw in three easy but deep breaths into your abdomen, just above your navel . . . then allow your breathing to return to a normal easy breath and just notice your breathing in and your breathing out . . . Then, this time I want you to visualise or to remember a beautiful and peaceful place. It can be a place from your imagination, or from a film, a memory from your childhood, or a holiday memory. Imagine yourself lying or sitting in this beautiful place, a place where you feel comfortable, safe, and able to relax. Notice the colours and shapes in this place and take a moment to breathe in the beauty of it . . . Notice any sounds in this place and breathe in the peace of it . . . Now, feel your body relaxing as you connect with this place and feel a part of it . . . Imagine that you are completely held and supported by this place . . . Then allow yourself to feel fully comfortable and connected with your body, allow yourself to feel that oneness with yourself and with your surroundings.

As you are beginning to feel comfortable and relaxed, I want you to imagine a golden ball of light about the size of a table tennis ball—sitting softly in the middle of your forehead. This light is the most powerful, brightest, golden light you can imagine. I want you to slowly move this golden ball of light into your head using your *in* breath . . . You will have complete control of where you take this golden ball of light within your body and you will move it with your *in* breathe, slowly and gently, around your body. Now, I would like you to connect with your body more deeply and search for anywhere in your body that is carrying unwanted tension, stress, or tiredness . . . Then with your *in* breath, gently and slowly move this golden ball of light to that place . . . When it reaches that place I want you to imagine this ball of light slowly rolling around being moved by your *in* breath all around that part of your body that is tense, stressed, or tired . . . As it moves around, notice the warm feeling that is left behind . . . Everywhere the golden ball of light touches becomes still and yet is also energised, creating an inner sparkle . . . Remember, you have complete control of moving this golden ball of light slowly and gently with your *in* breath. Stay in this area of your body that needs relaxing and keep the golden ball of light moving slowly round and round, moving it with your *in* breath, and take pleasure from the warmth and energy that is being left behind in this part of your body . . . This powerful golden light becomes brighter and brighter the more work you ask it to do for you . . . Stay in this area, rolling around the golden ball of light, slowly and gently as long as you need to, until you feel this part of your body is truly relaxed . . . Feel the warmth from this light radiating out into your whole body. When you feel ready to move on to another area of your body, connect deeply with your whole body and notice anywhere else that is carrying unwanted tension, stress, or tiredness . . . When you are ready, take this golden ball of light, with your *in* breath, slowly to that place and, as it moves through your body, notice the warmth that it leaves behind as it energises every part of you that it touches. It leaves behind it a warm energy and a relaxation. When you get to the next place that is tense, stressed or tired, again, roll this golden ball of light around in this area, moving it slowly with your *in* breath . . . Notice the warmth that is left behind from this light and the energy and warmth that it brings to every part of you that it touches . . . In this way the golden ball of light clears away all stress, tension, and tiredness and the warmth, relaxation, and energy radiates through your whole body . . . Feel your whole body relaxing even more deeply from the warmth of this powerful golden ball of light . . . Notice that this golden ball of light becomes brighter and stronger as it moves around your body . . . The power of this light is unlimited . . . Continue to connect with your body and notice any part of your body that is still carrying tension, stress, or tiredness . . . You can take this ball of light down to the tips of your fingers or to the tips of your toes, moving it gently and slowly through your body, with your *in* breath, wherever it needs to go. Feel the warmth, energy and relaxation that is left behind everywhere within you that is touched by this powerful healing light . . . You have complete control of the movement of this ball of light with your *in* breath. Let yourself feel this radiating out into your whole body and deeper still into your emotional self, into your mind, relaxing you and renewing your energy as tension, stress, and tiredness are completely cleared away . . . Again, with your *in* breath slowly and gently move this golden ball of light to those places you are discovering. As you move it slowly to these places feel the warmth and energy melt away all unwanted tension, stress, or tiredness, however old . . . Remember the light becomes brighter and stronger the more work you ask it to do . . . You have complete control of moving it around your body and you intuitively know the places where you most need to take it to. When you are ready, in your own time, prepare to take this golden ball of light back up into your head . . . With your *in* breath take your time and slowly and gently move this golden ball of light up into your head . . . Again as you move it through your body, feel the warmth radiating out from the brightness of the golden light, feel it radiating out into your body and enjoy the feeling of energy and relaxation that is left behind everywhere it has touched you . . . Finally, with your *in* breath, take the golden ball of light once more around your head or behind your eyes, which, so often become tense and tired . . . As you roll it around and around with your *in* breath, again enjoy the warmth, energy, and relaxation that it leaves behind . . . Then, when you are ready, with your *in* breath, gently push out the golden ball of light so that it ends up sitting in the middle of your forehead . . . Know that you can do this for yourself any time you feel anxious or stressed. Be aware of this special place of beauty and safety that you can return to any time, notice the colours, sounds, and peace of this place . . . Slowly, in your own time, come back into this room . . . Take your time, and open your eyes and notice a colour or a shape in the room to bring you back into the present moment . . . You can repeat this whenever you need to. Take a few moments to sit and just "be" with this relaxation that you have created . . . I always add the advice not to drive or work any machinery of any sort for at least twenty minutes after this kind of relaxation.

Lan-li slowly opens her eyes. She stretches and yawns a couple of times as she looks around the room.

L: That was so cool. I'm definitely going to do that one again.

C: I can let you have a printed copy of this and a couple of shorter relaxations. You could record it in your own voice so that you can listen to it and practice whenever you like.

L: Yes please.

C: I'll leave a copy in the office for you to pick up.

L: Thanks.

C: You can probably find other relaxations, meditations, and visualisa-tions to download onto your iPod, you can *choose* the ones you like best.

Lan-li reaches for her bag.

L: Thinking of "choosing" again. I brought something to show you. This is what I decided to buy for myself to celebrate my recovery.

Lan-li takes a white cardboard box out of her bag. She puts it on her lap and opens it. From the tissue paper in the box she takes out a beautifully decorated silver hand mirror. It makes me smile and I feel tears in my eyes at the appropriateness of this wonderful gift to herself. I am going to miss working with this shiny young woman.

C: What a fantastic gift to yourself . . . You've become pretty good at choosing.

Lan-li draws a card out of her bag and hands it to me.

L: Well this might just remind you.

Lan-li passes me a white envelope with my name on it. I open it and inside is a card and on the outside of the card, which she's made herself, is a picture of the mirror made with tin foil. Underneath she's written in silver pentel, "The (Looking) Glass is Now Full".

C: That is the best thank you I could have wished for. You have been such a fantastic person to work with. I feel privileged to have been able to get to know you . . . for both of us to get to know you. I know you will be successful at whatever you choose to do because you've shown yourself to be very willing to make more constructive choices that enable you to realise your potential.

L: I'm very grateful to you for the work we've done together. You've made it easy for me and I've felt you've held a mirror up to me that I could finally see into. Thank you.

C: I don't think you will need to, but do feel that you can always contact me again and have another session at a later date if you want to.

L: I hope I won't need to come back but it's good to know there is some-where I can come if I need to.

I walk Lan-li to the door and we give each other a hug.

CASE TWO

Shirley and David's story: finding the heart

Relationship breakdown

Often we are attracted to life partners for the very qualities that can eventually become difficult to us. There can be an unconscious positive and negative fit that is being worked out in any relationship. The specific example used in this chapter is a couple in a heterosexual relationship, but some of these issues are equally commonplace in homosexual relationships. It is common in relationships for us to become "stuck" or "polarised" in terms of power or control, to become preoccupied by a need to be "right" and to make the other person "wrong". Fear plays a part in this, a fear of not wanting to be controlled by others, a fear of being out of control, a fear of not being good enough, a fear of being vulnerable. What can help us get beyond this "attack" or "defend" position is for us to begin to understand how the other person feels and how we feel ourselves. It is more difficult to stay being "right" when you can see beyond the logical arguments to the feelings underneath. This understanding increases the trust in the relationship, which makes it easier to move forward to a resolution.

Our partners, whether heterosexual or homosexual, can be our greatest teachers about ourselves and about relationships. It can be our inherent differences that enable us to work together creatively and build something authentic and successful.

One of the things that has enabled me, as a counsellor, to have genuine empathy for my clients, is when a client has had the courage to risk *trusting* me with their innermost feelings. It is humbling and almost impossible not to have compassion for someone who is able to be truly vulnerable and "human" and serves to remind me that we are much more similar than we are different when it comes to feelings. I imagine that there is nowhere in the world where people have not at some time experienced, loss or sadness; anger or frustration; fear or terror; shame or guilt and, it is to be hoped, at some point, joy and happiness; unless of course there is a medical reason for someone not being able to experience their feelings fully.

Brief assessment summary

Clients: Shirley, thirty-eight and a playgroup supervisor and David, forty-one and an accountant. Married fifteen years. Two children, Matthew ten and Katie eight.

Presenting problem: Serious marital difficulties due to a fundamental disagreement about whether or not to send their son and eventually their daughter away to boarding school as weekly boarders. Talking about divorce.

Family background:

Shirley: mother, black British, came over from Trinidad as a teenager, living; father, white British, Londoner, died just over a year ago; two sisters, Pat, thirty-five and Dorothy thirty-three.

Religious affiliation: occasional Baptist church as a child.

David: mother, white British, living; father, white British, living; one brother, Adam, forty-five.

Religious affiliation: occasional Church of England as a child.

Neither have had any previous co-habiting relationships.

Neither have had any previous therapy/counselling.

Referral: self referred.

First session of counselling

Before going down to the waiting room to meet Shirley and David Robertson, I had read their assessment notes with some concern. From their body language, I can see that this will not be an easy first session. They sit opposite one another. David's arms are tightly folded and Shirley is protectively hugging the handbag on her lap; both of them look out of the window. I introduce myself, shake hands with them, and lead the way down the hallway to my room. I had laid out two chairs part facing each other and part facing my own seat, which had my diary on. It was the nearest I could make it to a small circle. I invite them to sit down. Shirley folds herself gracefully into the chair nearest to the window. She sits upright, and keeps her handbag on her lap. David sits nearest the door and when he rests one foot on his other knee, he seems all legs. He is white with short brown hair, clean shaven, and looks younger than forty-one. Shirley is an attractive mixed race woman of thirty-eight with short, curly, black hair, large silver earrings, and a silver charm bracelet. She is wearing narrow silver framed glasses. They avoid eye contact with each other. Shirley looks down at her bag and David looks expectantly at me.

> *Counsellor*: Well, I know you've had a four week wait since your assessment with Michael, so maybe you'd like to tell me how things are between you now.

I look at both of them, unsure who is going to talk first. Shirley looks out of the window.

> *David*: To be honest, things are about as bad as they can be.

I look over at Shirley to elicit a response from her.

> *Shirley*: We're hardly talking except around the children and if we had a spare bedroom, one of us would be sleeping in it.

> C: I'm sorry about that . . . I hope we can work together to find a way through this . . . I'd like to start by asking both of you what you want to get from these five sessions. Shirley, what about you, what would you like to achieve from this?

> S: I'd like David to let go of this ridiculous idea of splitting up our family by our ten-year-old son Matthew being forced to go to a school far away from his family, friends, and everything that's familiar to him . . . there are some things that are more important than education . . . that money can't buy.

C: What would you like to achieve from this process David?

David puts both feet on the floor and sits upright in his seat.

D: I'm being made out to be the baddy here but I want the best for my family. I want Shirley to see sense . . . I've worked hard to build up a successful company and I can provide the best education for our children . . . Matthew would come home at weekends and be with the family. He's a sociable boy and would make friends easily and there are countless advantages in the facilities at my old school that he won't get in a London school . . . it's in beautiful surroundings . . . the level of education is excellent, not just academically, but in music, art, and sport. It would assure him of a good university place and a successful future when it comes to a job.

C: I'm hearing that both of you want the other person to change. How long have you been struggling with this issue?

D: We've been talking about it and not talking about it for about nine months and the time has come to make a decision, for Matthew's sake . . . for everyone's sake.

S: The truth is that David wants Matthew to be a carbon copy of himself . . . he thinks it did him good to go to boarding school, despite a lot of unhappiness which he's conveniently forgotten. I think it's an inhuman system . . . and it's not just me that thinks that . . . it goes against eleven points in the UN Law on the Rights of the Child according to an article I read . . .

D: For God's sake Shirley, that article was so biased . . .

S: . . . and true . . . both David's parents went through the same type of school system. They wanted the same for their children, but David married and had children with me and I'm not like his parents or like him. I have my own views and I come from a different culture and background where family life matters more than education. He's my child too . . . he's happy with his friends and would be happy going on to the local comprehensive with them.

D: I understand that it's harder for Shirley but she must see that Matthew comes first and what gives him an advantage in the world has to be our priority as parents. You must see that.

David looks at me wanting me to agree with him.

S: You can be such a pompous arse, *"You must see that"* . . .

Shirley's eyes are flashing and she's pointing her finger towards David as she mimics his voice accentuating his Home Counties English accent. I intervene.

> C: Underneath the frustration and anger you have towards each other, I believe that you both genuinely want what's best for Matthew. I know how painful it is when a couple can't agree on something as important as this. I'm happy to work with you to find a solution which is what you've come here to do, together . . . Let's take a step back and take some time to look at your relationship, family values, what you share, and what the differences are. Then it may be possible for you to find some points of agreement and compromise that could even lead to new options you haven't considered . . . Are you both willing to take some time to understand more about how you got to this place before we look at how to resolve it?

> D: Yes of course.

> S: If we don't find a solution, I can't see us staying together, so yes.

David turns angrily to face Shirley.

> D: Then what happens to the family life you say you value so much?

> S: It's already being destroyed by you.

> C: Let's hope it doesn't come to that although I'm willing to look at both options with you. Right now, I'd like to understand more about each of you and your families, where you came from, and how you got together. Are you willing to start there and see where we get to?

They both nod.

> C: Perhaps you'd begin by telling me about how you met, what attracted you to each other, and what made you decide to get married.

I looked at both of them giving them the chance to decide who goes first.

> D: I used to go and see the bands at the Art College where Shirley was studying. One of my friends had a younger brother studying there . . . we used to dance together and just "clicked". I liked the fact that she always had something to say . . . I was quite shy then . . . with girls . . .

> S: Having gone to an "all boys' school" . . . he had no idea about women . . .

> C: Let's stay with the past for a bit Shirley . . .

S: Okay . . . sorry.

D: She's right, I didn't have much of a clue and Shirley was easy to talk to . . . she loved music and dancing with a passion, knew a lot about jazz and blues . . . she encouraged me to play in a jazz band. I knew London pretty well but she showed me places, galleries, and clubs that I didn't know existed. Although I enjoyed my studies as an accountant, music and art have always been important to me.

C: What made you decide that you wanted to marry Shirley?

D: . . . She was creative and made everything more than it was before . . . I think she did the same with me . . . she put people . . . me . . . at my ease. I felt I could do anything when I was around her. She encouraged me to start the business with Will and Grant straight after qualifying and helped us to set up some of the volunteer work with local groups . . . I got on with her family and enjoyed the get-togethers . . . music was part of that too. It just felt the right thing to do for us to get married . . . just as it feels the right thing for Matthew to go to my old school.

Shirley raises her eyebrows and raises her arms at his comment so I just shake my head and ignore it. He looks a bit sheepish.

C: Thank you David . . . what about you Shirley . . . what attracted you to David and what made you decide to marry him?

S: As he said, we shared a lot . . . dancing . . . art . . . gigs . . . mutual friends. My family liked him . . . he couldn't do any wrong in their eyes. David reminded me a bit of dad, ambitious but gentle and kind. I liked the fact that he wanted to help people who were less fortunate. He had a strange and appealing mix of confidence and quietness. He was different from a lot of the guys I knew at Art College who could be a bit airy fairy. I liked the fact that David knew his own mind . . . that he wanted to start his own business but that it wasn't all about making money, it was also about doing something for the community. David was very straightforward and I knew right from the beginning that he was the person I wanted to spend the rest of my life with.

C: I see from your assessment that you've been married for fifteen years. What have you most appreciated and valued about each other in that time together?

D: I used to feel supported by Shirley and I used to be able to talk through things to do with work with her and she'd come up with some good ideas. She encouraged me to try new things, to take risks. She's a great mum and she organises a lot of what goes on at home without it seeming as if it's a problem. She organises our social life, holidays, family outings, school events, birthdays. I appreciate that I just turn up and Shirley has it all under control. Sometimes, I don't know how she's had the time because she's there for the children as well. Mainly, she cooks but we both muck in to clear up when people are coming over to visit. She makes an effort to look nice and wear a sexy perfume. We share a taste in music and used to listen to a lot of music at home. She takes the time to make the table look nice with flowers or a decoration and candles.

I look over towards Shirley

S: David's always been a good provider for us and he works very hard. He doesn't do work on the house himself but he has good contacts to find the right person to mend something if it's broken. We used to discuss things together and David used to include me in decision making, even if sometimes he had the final say. We haven't very often disagreed about the big things up until recently. He used to talk about work and include me in what he was doing. He has a good sense of humour and we've usually been able to see the funny side of most things, eventually. He's great with the children at showing them things and I've enjoyed watching him teaching Katie how to play the guitar, he knows how to make it fun for her. He used to be genuinely interested in me talking about the people at work especially if there was a problem with one of the children. When we've had family or friends over to the house, David helps make everything go smoothly as he's very sociable and a good host. I used to enjoy cuddling up to him at night when he was affectionate and we were getting on well.

C: What do you think are the things that have been most difficult to accept in each other since being married?

Both of them look down, not wanting to be first to answer but David starts.

D: To be honest, this whole debacle about Matthew has been a mess and has made me seriously question whether I made the right decision all those years ago. I couldn't have foreseen that Shirley would be so stubborn about something that is such an obvious advantage for our son . . .

S: In your view, you pompous arse . . . God you just piss me off with your, "*oh so superior attitude*". You never listen to anyone else. You're so arrogant . . . I can't stay here and listen to your crap . . .

Shirley leans forward and has her hands on the arms of the chair ready to stand up.

C: I hear that you're very angry Shirley, but I'd like you to stay. Maybe we need to avoid the subject of Matthew's schooling for the moment. I'd like to understand more about your relationship history and your family backgrounds. So, will you both agree to suspend *any* comments just for now that refer to your children's schooling?

I look to each of them and reluctantly they both nod.

C: Maybe we can come back to the aspects that you've found difficult in your relationship. Perhaps, today, you could tell me more about your families. Shirley, tell me a bit about your family background.

S: Well, mum and her sister, Mary, were born in Trinidad and as young teenagers came over here with my grandparents in the Sixties. They all found it hard to settle as it was so different from home and it was cold. They'd left sunshine and a large family and lots of friends behind. It was hardest for Mary who was the oldest and after she trained as a nurse, she went back to Trinidad. Mum settled down in London and met dad at work and after they got married he moved in with her, grandma, and grandpa. Dad was a Londoner through and through and he used to say, "I'm a *real* cockney born within the sound of Bow bells". He was an engineer with London Transport . . . he was white . . . his parents weren't happy with mum but came around when they had children.

C: Do you mean because she was black?

S: Yes, they were disappointed that he married a black woman.

C: How was that for you?

S: They were nice to us kids and they ended up accepting their "coloured" family. They were proud of us when we did well at school. The area that they lived in changed a lot from when they were kids. They're very open about how difficult it was for them to adjust to all the immigrants moving into Hackney during their life time. They were afraid that they'd be the only white people left in their road.

C: Did you encounter racism at school or elsewhere?

S: No more than anything else, kids will pick on anything that's "different". The school I went to in Brixton was multi-cultural and the teachers were a "mixed bag". There were some nasty comments from neighbours but I understood about them because of dad's parents. Sometimes it got to me but mostly it didn't bother me. I knew I belonged to my family, if you know what I mean, and that made me feel safe.

C: Is it a problem for you, me being a white counsellor?

S: No, I don't think so. Maybe, I'm a bit concerned that you would take David's part about Matthew's schooling.

C: Will you let me know if you think that's happening at any point?

S: Yes I will . . . thanks . . . that helps.

C: Carry on telling us about your family.

S: Well, after mum and dad married, they lived with my grandparents in Brixton and that's where me and my two sisters were born. When I was about five, Mary came to live with us. She'd gone back to Trinidad before I was born, got married, and had several miscarriages, and then divorced . . . don't know if that was because she couldn't have children. Anyway, she came to live with us just before my sister Dorothy, was born. I was five and my sister Pat was three. She was a bit like another mum.

C: What was good about your growing up and what was most difficult?

S: Well the same thing really. I loved having loads of people around to hang out with but they'd also tell you what to do all the time. I craved privacy but liked having family around too. I got on well with mum and gran. Gramps lost his job and began to drink too much and it was like living with two people. We were scared if he got drunk 'cos you never knew what he was capable of. He'd be fun when sober but drunk, he'd shout and hit out at us . . . unless dad was around but then they used to argue. It was a relief when we moved into our own house. I was ten. Then I was expected to look after my sisters while mum was working at home . . . she'd been a bookkeeper before having me . . . after we moved she went back to work outside the home as a school dinner lady but she worked at home as a bookkeeper. She's a teacher's assistant now but still keeps her hand in doing people's books. She always wanted to be a teacher. The old house was converted into two flats after we moved out. Gran and Gramps stayed in the one until they died and then it was let out. Mary moved into the other. Then, after dad died, just over a year ago, mum moved back into Gran's flat, so there they are back in the same house again. My dad's mum is still alive but she's in a nursing home that specialises in dementia, luckily for her she doesn't realise that dad's dead. She's the only grandparent still alive now.

C: Is there anything else you'd like me to know about you that might help us here?

S: Only how important family is to me. I enjoy my job as a playgroup supervisor and I think I'm good at it . . . probably 'cos I did look after my sisters, although I resented it a bit at the time. I never found my job as a designer, after Art College, nearly as satisfying as having children or running the playgroup. When Matthew and Katie are older, I want to retrain as a teacher, probably primary school. I want to continue to use my art to teach children . . . that and making a home is important to me. I can't think of anything else I'd rather do.

C: Thanks Shirley, I do hear how important family is to you.

I turn to David and he looks thoughtful.

C: Before I ask you to tell us about your own childhood David, you're probably aware of most of what Shirley's told us but how did you feel listening to her today?

D: To be honest, I felt moved. I suppose I haven't been listening to much that Shirley's been saying recently and well, it just reminded me of who she is and where she's come from . . . that's all.

C: What do you experience Shirley to hear David say this?

S: I'm glad if he can hear where I'm coming from.

C: So David tell us a bit about yourself. What was good about your childhood and what was difficult?

D: Well, home was very comfortable. There were the four of us. My mother was a head teacher and very efficient at organising the household . . . a wonderful cook . . . always there in the holidays. She'd be great at birthday treats and parties . . . she read bedtime stories to us. She had a social circle of friends and their children would come and play. We had a large garden that we'd get lost in for hours at a time. It was pretty idyllic. My father was an accountant in the City and so would be home quite late but we'd do things as a family at weekends. We'd have picnics, visit places like Richmond Park, Kew Gardens, and Hampton Court. We'd go on holiday together usually in France or Cornwall, by the sea. He'd take me up to see rugby matches and he'd take my brother Adam fishing, so we both had time with him. Adam and I had different friends as we got older but when we were young we used to make camps. We played card games as a family and, of course, music. My mother played piano and I played clarinet and guitar. Adam was tone deaf so didn't play anything.

C: What was most difficult for you?

D: Well, Adam was a bit of a bully . . .

S: A bit, David?

D: Well, okay he was quite cruel actually. He was four years older than me and he was very jealous. Any toys I got . . . he'd *accidentally* break them . . . the first one I remember was when I had an electric train set for Christmas and he *accidentally* walked on the engine and broke it . . . that was repeated with all sorts of things . . . model aircraft, CD's, remote control cars . . . I learnt to keep out of his way. When he was in a good mood, he was exciting to play with and he'd make fantastic camps in the garden and then out of the blue he'd lose it. I didn't see much of him at school but ironically his reputation stopped me ever getting bullied at school. I began as a weekly boarder and then at fifteen, I decided to board termly. It was sociable and there was always something to do that was interesting. I had great friends. The sport and music was exceptional. I was happy there.

C: Is there anything else you'd like us to know that might help us here?

D: Not really . . . to be honest, I feel I was exceptionally fortunate and had so many experiences that have helped me . . . that's why I want Matthew and Katie to benefit from that as well.

C: Well, I can certainly understand why school was important to you and I wonder how you feel Shirley about what David's told us.

S: I feel sad for David, although he's saying he was fortunate, I think Adam was really horrible to him and sometimes, he still is. I think it's awful not to be able to trust your own brother.

I can see David's eyes begin to tear up but he quickly controls himself.

C: It's horrible to be bullied . . . It's valuable for me to hear more about you both. What do you experience David, to hear what Shirley has just said?

D: I feel a bit sad about the distance between Adam and I, and I feel sad about the distance between Shirley and myself at the moment.

C: What do you think has made it difficult for you to be able to come to some resolution about this issue of Matthew's schooling?

D: We both feel very strongly and our anger towards each other has stopped us from hearing the other person.

S: Sometimes, it feels like that there's a power struggle over who is more "right".

C: In order to move forward with this, it seems important to get past all that's getting in the way. So I'd like to suggest that you tell each other how you're feeling at the moment about this and about what you need *but* from an "*I*" position not from an accusatory "*You*" position. I've found that a good way of doing this is to use a kind of formula . . . something like: *I feel . . . about . . . my idea/fantasy/perception is that . . . What I need for myself is . . .* Also, I think it would be valuable for you to talk directly to each other. Would you be willing to do that?

I look over at each of them and they nod and look over at each other.

C: Who's going to start?

S: I will.

C: Thank you . . . I'd like you to move your chairs slightly so that you are squarely facing each other and I need you to say this directly to David and for him to listen and respond in a way that tells you that he's heard you. So it's: *I feel . . . about . . . my idea/fantasy/perception is that . . . What I need for myself is . . .* Is that okay?

S: Yeah.

They both move their chairs until they are facing each other. Shirley puts her bag down on the floor, looks at me a bit anxiously and then faces David. He sits well back in his seat.

S: . . . I feel . . . so . . . angry inside . . .

Tears fill her large brown eyes and she wipes them away. She picks up her handbag and searches for a tissue, ignoring the box of tissues on the small table next to her. She wipes her eyes and nose before she begins again.

S: . . . No . . . I feel devastated . . . devastated . . . at the thought of Matthew leaving us all to go to *that* school . . . my fear is that he'll be lonely and hurt . . . that he'll change . . . become a stranger to us . . . to Katie . . . to mum and Mary . . . to Pat and Dorothy . . . his cousins . . . his friends . . . What I need for myself . . . is for you to understand that this is wrong for me, it's against everything I believe in, everything I am . . . I haven't grown up with this and . . . it's . . . it's alien to me . . . The part of you that's a product of that school is alien to me . . . I need you to hear that I can't let this happen to Matthew . . . to Katie . . . to us . . . to any of us.

Shirley cries again and blows her nose. David looks shocked but does not comfort her. The silence frames the pain that she expresses which sits in the centre of the room.

D: . . . I don't think I've realised how deeply you feel.

S: . . . I don't think I knew how deeply I felt either but I do.

C: Thank you Shirley. Could you tell Shirley how you feel David, using the same format: *I feel . . . about . . . my idea/fantasy/perception is that . . . What I need for myself is . . .?*

D: Yes.

David rubs the bristles on his jaw back and forth with the flat of his hand and looks over at Shirley.

D: I feel . . . I feel confused . . . about what's right . . . I want to do the very best for Matthew and Katie . . . I want to do the best for everyone . . . I want to be a good father and a good person . . .

David rubs his jaw again, hard.

D: What I need for myself . . . is not to lose you and the family . . . but I need to be heard too . . . I know what the school is like and I've always assumed that our children will go there . . . their other cousins go there . . . I need you to trust me.

S: I hear what you're saying . . . I know that you want the best for them . . . but I can't agree with you that this is the best thing. Maybe there's another way.

C: Thank you both. I appreciate that you have begun to make an effort to listen to each other today despite your very different views on the issue of Matthew's education and I don't think you would be here if you didn't want to find a positive way forward. I'm aware that it's time for us to end for today and I have a suggestion of some homework that I hope you may consider doing during the week. My suggestion is that you take yourselves off this week to do something together which doesn't involve talking about this whole thing . . . maybe dancing, cinema, an exhibition. It seems important that you spend some prime time together doing something as a couple. I know that you want to make a decision sooner rather than later but I think it could be valuable to take the pressure off yourselves for the time being. Strangely, this is the opposite of what a counsellor might be expected to suggest.

D: Right now, that feels like a relief.

S: I agree, even though it hardly seems possible.

C: I do think what you've shared today will prove to be something we can build on in the weeks to come. It seems to me to be important to take the pressure off at home for a few weeks while we're looking at it here together.

We make an appointment for the following week and as they walk out the door I let out a large sigh of relief. The tension in the room has been rolled up tight.

Second session of counselling

When I go to collect Shirley and David from the waiting room, I find David anxiously pacing in the hallway and he tells me that Shirley is going to be a few minutes late. By the time he sits down, in the same seat as last week, there is a knock on the door and Shirley has arrived, out of breath and apologetic.

> C: While you take a few moments Shirley, I'll ask David, if you were able to put aside your differences this week and do something together.

> D: As it happened, the children were both busy on Saturday afternoon, so we did set off to go to an exhibition at the Royal Academy but while we were waiting in the queue, an old school friend of mine came by and that sparked off an argument . . . It was a bit embarrassing as Roger was a bit of prat and when I introduced him to Shirley, he vaguely mumbled "hello" and carried on talking to me . . .

> S: He was downright rude, barely acknowledged me, and talked over you, just wanted to tell you how successful he was . . . pompous sod . . . and you let him get away with it. How could you want Matthew to be educated to turn out like that?

> D: I have to admit he was rude . . .

> C: That was a really unfortunate thing to happen for both of you, especially when you were making a big effort to do something together and there you are faced with the issue head on . . . I'm sorry that happened and although I can understand why you were angry Shirley, school friends from any school can behave like that.

> S: I know it was bad timing but it really pissed me off.

> C: Did you end up going into the exhibition?

> D: We didn't, but that was mainly because the queue was moving so slowly that it was getting too late to see it properly. The *Bronze* exhibition is an important spectacle, worth doing properly. We eventually decided to visit the permanent exhibition at the National Portrait Gallery instead

and despite the fact that we were a bit moody with each other, it turned out to be enjoyable. We haven't done anything like that for a long time.

S: I needed to get away and walk off my anger but it was still good to do something together for the first time in ages.

C: It sounds as if this conflict has stopped you from doing things that you enjoy. As communication between you has been difficult, I wonder if it might be helpful that what you talk about in this session be addressed between you again. Would you mind turning your chairs so that you are more directly facing each other?

They, somewhat reluctantly, turn their chairs towards each other.

C: I think it might be valuable for you to tell each other what it is that you are missing in your relationship at the moment. What do you think?

D: Yes, I can see that.

S: Okay.

C: So who would like to start?

D: I don't mind going first if that's okay with you Shirley?

S: That's fine.

D: One of the things I'm missing Shirley is the physical comfort but also that good feeling about coming home . . . that ease and sense of being "at home" and being able to relax with you and the children at the end of the day. Although we each do things with the children, we do it separately. We go out and see friends occasionally but everything we do feels tense . . . most of all I miss laughing with you and seeing you smile.

C: What about you Shirley?

S: Well, I miss talking with you about my day. I don't really know what's going on for you at work . . . there's a tension when we're being polite in front of the children . . . I feel as if I'm having to force down an anger that's just below the surface waiting to bubble up. This has gone on too long for me so that I hardly feel as if I'm myself anymore . . . it's a bit like I used to feel around Gramps when he was drinking.

C: How long has it been like this?

D: About eight or nine months, maybe longer.

C: Are you still having a sexual relationship?

D: Oh no . . . that stopped way back.

S: We haven't made love since we were on holiday last summer, since our first real blow up about all this.

C: How was your sexual relationship before then?

D: It was good . . . at least I think it was.

David looks a bit anxiously at Shirley.

C: Could you continue to talk about this more directly with each other again.

D: I've enjoyed our sexual relationship before all this started but I don't want to talk for you. Did you enjoy it?

S: It was good for me as well. I've enjoyed our sexual life together and the fact that we could talk about it then but it was a part of a relationship which doesn't seem to exist for us anymore.

D: I feel sad about that and I wish we could find a way back to that intimacy. I understand that we need to sort out these differences.

S: I feel let down and angry with you David. I need some kind of willingness to compromise . . . some way to move forward.

C: How sad for you both, it sounds painful to be in this position. It makes it important that we find a way through it. What do you need to say to each other about this?

S: I feel stuck in something that hasn't been of my making . . . I guess we didn't talk about education beyond primary school and this came at me out of the blue . . . It started when you told me that you'd put Matthew's name down for your old school, when he was a baby, without any discussion with me at all . . . I'd no idea. We've gone along happily enough with some conflicts and some real struggles which we've managed to sort out . . . but this came up only a few months after dad's death . . . I was reeling from that . . . I was vulnerable and I couldn't believe you could be so secretive and inflexible, I still can't . . . I've lost my trust in you, and I'm not even sure who you are any more.

D: To be honest Shirley . . . I didn't give it a thought after that initial contact with the school . . . I didn't see it would be a problem. I brought it up so that we could discuss it . . . I never thought it would be so contentious and go on this long . . . time's passed and it's just got worse for us to talk and the less we've talked, the further apart we've become. I felt bad about the timing but I had no control over that, it needs sorting out before Matthew changes school. I couldn't have imagined you being so stubborn and uncompromising, so maybe I don't trust you either.

C: It's very painful to lose trust in a marriage and the timing must have been particularly hard for you Shirley.

S: I've felt devastated . . . I've been supporting mum, who's obviously found dad's death hard to deal with. He was coming up for retirement and they'd planned a trip to Trinidad together . . . he had a heart attack at work and died before he got to hospital. It was a shock for her . . . for all of us. She's very brave and has just carried on with her life. We've all been there for her, Mary, Pat, and Dorothy when she can . . . including David, he's been good with her, looking after all the paperwork and practical things.

C: Can you tell me something about the way you've resolved other differences and disagreements in your relationship?

D: There haven't been a huge amount . . . I suppose the first difficulties arose in planning our wedding. My parents wanted us to have a more formal affair and Shirley wanted a relaxed family wedding . . . I felt a bit caught in the middle but we managed to find a compromise, didn't we?

S: It took a while, but yes, we did.

C: How did you manage that?

S: We got married in my family's Baptist church in Brixton, around the corner from our old house with their fantastic gospel choir. I hardly ever went to the church but mum went occasionally and Aunt Mary is a regular. She helps to run the choir and even my dad would go occasionally to hear them. We filled the church just with family and then had a lovely meal in a local Greek restaurant owned by friends. David's mum and dad loved the choir. Then, we had a more sophisticated summer party for friends and family at David's parent's house in a marquee in their garden later in the year, with a friend's jazz band playing, which my family also thoroughly enjoyed. It took some organising but everyone helped out.

C: It sounds as if you brought your two families together in a very positive way and it's lovely that music is something important for all of you.

S: The only real problem was that Adam and his family weren't able to or didn't want to come to the actual wedding . . . David had Grant and Will, both of his business partners as "best men" which was great fun . . . they're more like brothers really.

C: Was it hard for you that your brother didn't come to the church wedding David?

D: Oh, that's just Adam . . . he's an incredible snob and I'm afraid his wife, Melanie goes along with whatever he says . . . he agreed to be Master of Ceremonies at the summer party and enjoyed lording it over everyone.

D: Probably the biggest disagreement we've had to deal with was that Shirley wanted to have a larger family and I wanted to stop at two children . . . I suppose two felt natural for me having only one brother . . .

S: . . . and three felt natural for me . . . I would have been happy to have more . . . mum says that's why I run a playgroup . . . we talked it through a lot and it wasn't easy but it wasn't anywhere near as difficult as this.

D: I wanted to be able to afford to give our two children the best chance we could . . .

S: . . . but you never said anything about sending them away to school David.

D: . . . to be honest, I just took that for granted . . . that you'd want that too . . . when the time came.

C: Were there any other difficulties that arose in your marriage because of cultural or other differences?

S: I've found David to be quite cold sometimes and very independent . . . but there's something else, deeper, which I think comes from going away to school. I've read a few articles and a book or two about boarding schools since all this has come up and they talk about this. I think it applies to David.

C: Do you think you could say this to David directly and use the "formula", you used last week?

S: Okay, this is hard to say.

C: A reminder . . . *I feel . . . about . . . my idea/fantasy/perception is that . . . What I need for myself is . . .?*

S: Okay . . . sometimes, when you feel threatened by me in some way I don't understand, I feel shut out . . . rejected . . . I experience you changing from the warm loving man I married into a polite . . . cold . . . super-rational stranger. My experience is that I can't reach you and when I've tried to talk to you about this, you simply deny it and tell me I'm imag-ining it. This has happened when we've been getting on really well or when we have a problem. I believe, from what I've read, that this might be something you did to "survive" at school . . . I need you to take seri-ously what I've read about this and not ridicule it . . . I need you to listen to me . . . what I also need is for you to know that I'm really scared that this "switching off" could happen to Matthew and damage his relation-ships with us and his future relationships . . . this has been one of the hardest things for me to bear in our marriage.

D: It's just nonsense that this has anything to do with school . . . I need time to myself sometimes . . . that's normal and reasonable, isn't it?

David looks to me for support here. Shirley also looks to me for support.

C: What happens to you David when you hear that Shirley feels shut out and rejected at times?

D: To be honest, I think a lot of men need to get away from family life and the intensity of relationships sometimes . . . I spend a lot of time with clients at work and when I get home, I want to relax and do some things on my own . . . sometimes I find Shirley a bit intense.

C: Could you talk directly to Shirley about this, using as a basis the same "formula"?

David looked directly at Shirley but I noticed that he'd placed one foot back resting on his other knee which looked like a barrier or a protection.

D: Okay . . . I feel I want to escape and be on my own sometimes, espe-cially when you want to talk, *about us* and what I need is to be able to "switch off" from people, even family sometimes . . . I don't think this has anything to do with my background or schooling.

S: I know you need time on your own, so do I . . . I understand that very well, but you've been like this when we're on holiday, at weekends, and even after we've made love . . . I've thought about this a lot and I believe it happens when we've been particularly close or intimate.

D: I admit that I'm quite independent and perhaps that is something that comes from being away at school but I just can't see that as a bad thing.

S: I'm not saying it's a bad thing to have time on our own but it's the way you do it . . . it's fine for me if you tell me that you need time to yourself.

You quite often act first rather than talk to me about what you're doing ... like putting Matthew's name down at your old school, without me knowing anything about it ... I felt shut out.

C: I notice David that when you've talked about feelings, it can be more about an action ... like, you wanting to escape and last session you talked about feeling "confused" which might be more a state of mind ... do you find it difficult to identify or express your feelings?

D: I suppose I'm more familiar with thoughts and actions ... when I talk about wanting to escape, I suppose I'm feeling a bit overwhelmed ... stressed.

C: So would that be fear?

D: Maybe it is ... I suppose I do see it as a weakness to talk about fear.

C: Can you understand that for a young boy of eleven, staying away from home around many other boys that it might be a way of surviving, not to show *weakness* in that way?

D: Maybe ... I don't really remember much about my first year or two at school ... I know I did well academically and enjoyed the sport. I made friends easily enough ... but I don't really remember how I felt about it all.

C: Do you remember how it felt to go back home at weekends?

D: Not really ... I think it was a bit strange at first ... I don't think I went home for the first few weeks for some reason and then I thought it was all a bit quiet at home ... I was probably relieved to go back to school.

C: Were you ever angry with your parents for sending you away?

D: No never ... I knew it was a privilege ... I'd expected it ... wanted to be like Adam.

C: I have to say that I've worked with some adults who did find the adjustment to being away at school quite difficult but one of the hardest things is that it is thought to be just that ... a privilege. For some people it can be hard to express any negative feelings about something that parents make enormous sacrifices to do for their children. What do you think about that?

D: Of course I knew some boys who were unhappy and some didn't "stay the course" but there were compensations.

C: Do you think that Shirley may have a point that part of surviving so well, as you obviously did, might have led to you becoming more independent than is sometimes helpful in an intimate relationship like marriage?

D: Maybe . . . I can see what you're saying . . . perhaps I've taken for granted Shirley doing the feelings in the marriage . . . she's so much better than me at talking about things like that. I do leave it to her.

David turns back towards Shirley.

D: I know you've told me before that you feel lonely sometimes . . . I suppose I haven't really known how to deal with that.

S: I thought it was my fault, being used to lots of family around that I was being a bit too needy.

D: I know you've spoken to me before about me being hard to reach and I've totally denied it and even blamed you . . . will you persevere with me and tell me when I'm doing that next time?

S: Okay, if you're willing to listen.

D: I'm not going to forget that we've discussed it here.

S: You switch off from the children sometimes as well . . . I think that hurts me more than when you are distant from me.

D: Do I? I'm sorry . . . I don't think I realise when I'm doing it . . . I don't want to be distant from you or the children . . . I want to change this . . . will you help me?

S: Of course, I don't want to throw away all that we do have but you have to stop fighting me . . . I'm not your enemy.

D: Do I really treat you like that?

S: It feels like that sometimes.

C: Is there anyone in your family Shirley who you felt was distant from you?

S: I suppose dad would become distant when we disagreed and I'd have to apologise . . . he stopped talking to me completely for months when I applied to Art College . . . he wanted me to go to university. He'd been frustrated that his parents couldn't afford him to go. He'd wanted to be a proper engineer and his teachers encouraged him to go to university but even with grants in those days, he couldn't afford it. Mum stood up for me and helped me pay for art materials and books. We resolved it eventually but I felt I'd let him down . . . it really took until he saw my degree exhibition for him to understand what it meant to me. I think when David goes quiet and withdraws, it does take me back to that time and I feel as if I've done something wrong.

D: I didn't know that.

S: When we talk about Matthew and the school, it brings up deep feelings of self-doubt for me from the past . . . but I also trust what I feel about it.

C: I think you've both shared a lot today and I appreciate how open you've been to listening to each other. As its time to finish, I'd like to suggest that you continue to do something together which reminds you of what you enjoy about being together. Also, I'd like to suggest that, at home this week, you each write a list of possible alternative options that you might be willing to consider in addition to your obvious strongly held preferences. It may involve, other schools, moving house, moving country, changing jobs, even the most outlandish ideas which you haven't dared to think about. It would be useful if you could then score each option on a scale of one to ten. If you would bring your lists with you next week we'll talk more about that here. Are you willing to do that?

D: To be honest, I have some reluctance but I can see that it's a way of moving forward and so I'd be willing to see what we can come up with.

S: I feel relieved about thinking of other options.

We make an appointment for the following week, both of them in their electronic diaries and me in my old fashioned Filofax. We all stand up and I shake hands with each of them on the way out. There is the beginning of a new warmth between them this time.

Third session of counselling

I go down to the waiting room and David and Shirley are not talking but they are sitting next to each other. Shirley looks smart in her navy trouser suit and turquoise blouse and David is casually dressed as usual in a jacket and open necked shirt. Shirley picks up her handbag and they follow me down the hallway. They sit in their usual seats.

C: So, how would you like to use today?

D: Well, I think you'll be pleased with us as we organised for the children to spend Saturday with Shirley's sister Pat and her family and we went back to the Royal Academy to see the exhibition, *Bronze*, and we made it round the whole thing this time.

I smile at them both.

C: That's great. Did you enjoy it?

S: It was fantastic, beautiful lighting and dramatic settings. Do you know the spiders by Louise Bourgeois?

C: I do. I loved her giant spider that was in the Tate Modern entrance hall.

S: Well, they had one of her small spiders set on a bright white background which showed off its shadow and had an interesting effect. The animal pieces were special, a beautiful horses head, and there was a lovely African head from the fourteenth century, and Buddha from the sixth century . . . so much to admire. There was a whole section which showed how extraordinarily complex it was to cast the bronze models and all the various techniques and processes involved. It was a real joy. It's ages since we've taken the time to do that and yet it's what we did all the time when we were going out.

D: There was a great atmosphere and everything was perfectly positioned, I don't think they could have done it better. I admired the Chariot of the Sun from Denmark and King Seuthes, such expressive eyes and incredibly well preserved. I enjoyed Shirley's enthusiasm and her knowledge . . . It was excellent.

C: You both look energised by this. It would be good for you to continue to build time together as a couple again. It seems as if you've allowed this conflict to dominate your life together . . . Did you manage to do a list of alternative ideas about Matthew's education?

Shirley reaches down into her handbag and takes out a handwritten sheet. David takes a sheet of typed paper out of his jacket pocket.

C: Have you shared them with each other?

S: No.

C: Do you want to take it in turns to go through your whole list or take one option at a time?

D: I think it'd be good to take each option at a time. What do you think?

David asks Shirley.

S: I agree. Do you want to go first?

D: Okay.

I suggest that they move their seats back into a position that is opposite each other so they can again communicate more directly.

C: What I suggest is that you read out each option and tell us what score you gave. You could discuss it briefly here and then maybe you can find some options that you would find useful to discuss or research further at home together during this coming week. What do you think?

They both nodded and I looked to David to begin.

D: Obviously the first one on my list was the option of my old school.

Weekly boarder. Robertson family tradition. Everyone's done very well—excellent education, good career prospects, wide variety of musical, sporting, and creative extracurricular activities. School in beautiful wooded countryside for walks. Matthew would still see his friends and family at weekends. There is a sister school for Katie only a few miles away. They would have an excellent education and ex-pupils have best choices of university place including Oxford and Cambridge.—Score 10.

S: I'll read my comments out on that one shall I?

C: Yes do.

S: David's school: this isn't an option for me. An all boy's boarding school has the wrong atmosphere and ethos. For me, it has to be a proper co-ed school, where Matthew and Katie can become a part of the same school. Having a nearby sister school isn't the same. I don't want Matthew to grow up feeling convinced of his own superiority, as a man and as an elite public school boy so that he could lose his friends and caring for others. I don't want him in a system that puts ambition and achievement above love and family life. I want him to grow up being comfortable with the women in his life.—Score 0.

D: Come on Shirley, you can't honestly give it 0.

S: That's what I think David.

D: What does that say about what you think of me?

S: I love you David but, as I said last week, it's been very hard for me to reach the real you which I think has been squashed by the polite public school boy and I don't want that for Matthew or Katie.

D: You've certainly enjoyed the benefits of my education and success, financially and in other ways, in our life together.

S: I appreciate that you're very successful and a great provider but the cost has been high. I want more balance for our children, something in between what we both had. We're from different cultures and different classes and ideally I want our children to find a way that connects with the two of us. They can have both. We do.

C: That's a good point Shirley. You've chosen each other from different cultures and different classes and it sounds as if that's a richness in your life together. It would be ideal to find a school that you both think values those differences. Let's move on to the next option. Do you want to go next Shirley?

S: My favourite is obviously the nearest good comprehensive which is rated pretty highly.

The Broadway: this is the school where Matthew and his friends would normally go to from his present school and it's got a good reputation. It's got a good music and drama department, good art and design results, academically it's good and sports wise there's a link with a local athletics club. I'd be happy for Matthew and Katie to go here and its co-ed. It's not the best school in London, but I think it's an all-round good option and it's local.—Score 9.

D: My comments on that one are:

The Broadway. Good local school, a bit run down, some buildings need replacing. Good reputation for a local school. A bit hit and miss as regards extracurricular activities. Matthew would be with his friends from primary school and Katie could go there too. All the problems of a London inner city school in terms of money and development. Not very inspiring, "could do better".—Score 5.

S: That's unfair David, it's better than that.

D: Not for me.

C: So David do you want to go to the next one on your list?

D: We've both heard good things about St. John's from my colleague Grant who's children go there and are doing very well:

St. John's. Co-ed and private but not a boarding school. Very good results academically, an excellent reputation for art, music, and sport and it's right next to a large park. Worth looking into further.—Score 8.

S: I had a feeling that would be on your list, so I put it on mine too:

St. John's School : Grant's children go. Good reputation academically. Good art, drama, and music departments. Website looks good but it's a long journey across London. May mean that we'd have to move nearer the school. Co-ed, which is good. It means that Matthew and Katie would be uprooted from friends, but still in London.—Score 7.

C: It sounds as if this is one that could go on your list for more research and more discussion at home. What do you think?

S: I'd be willing to look at this and even to consider moving nearer.

D: That surprises me. I suppose I would be willing to look more at that too.

C: Shirley, your next option.

S: Well this is something completely different, you said to think more widely:

Sussex. Alternative system. Steiner Education. School near Dorothy and the Ashdown Forest. She has friends with children there. It sounds like the kind of school I wouldn't mind working in. Creative, free thinking, but good academic results. International school system. Mum's dream to live near the sea, maybe Sussex coast. Would she and Mary move—they've talked lots about living by the sea as children?—Score 7.

D: Actually, a client of mine had children in one of those schools somewhere near Gloucester and he was very positive about it. I don't know anything about it but I could ask him. It could be a bit airy fairy. On the other hand, we have a few large clients who've moved down to the Crawley area and one who's moved to Brighton. It's worth discussing further.

C: Any other options David?

D: Well one more . . . just a thought:

Exeter. Considered moving to Exeter when I left university but stayed in London. Walking and cycling around the moors, good schools, could set up my own business or open up a branch office there. Change—a new challenge, not necessarily for ever but while the children are pre-GCSE.— Score 7.

S: I don't fancy the West Country . . . it seems a long way from anyone we know but I'm open to discussing it.

C: Any other options from either of you?

S: My last one was rather unrealistic:

Trinidad: spend two or three years in Trinidad so that the children can connect with their roots, encourage mum and Mary to come with us.— Score 6.

D: That sounds a bit like my Exeter idea but I'm willing to discuss having an adventure; that's so off the map, it's appealing.

C: Any other ideas or comments you'd like to make?

S: Only that it feels a big relief to have other options on the table rather than a brick wall.

D: I don't mind discussing these options but I'm not prepared to give up on my first preference yet.

C: Being open enough to discuss any other options is a giant step forward. Have you discussed this whole issue with Matthew himself?

S: I asked David not to . . . it was creating such stress between us, I didn't feel it was fair to put Matthew in the middle . . . I think we need more agreement between us before we talk to him . . . of course the children know there's something wrong . . . they've heard us arguing and seen us not really talking to each other . . . but they trust that we sort things out between us. There is one thing though . . . I think that David's been unfair in the past six months in talking to Matthew about how exciting it is to go away to school. It feels as if he's been manipulating the situation with Matthew by telling him lots of stories about the fun he had at boarding school without being honest about any of the hardships. Whenever I've talked to David about it he denies he's doing this.

I look at David.

C: Is that true David?

D: I think it's natural for a father to talk to his son about his past experiences but I haven't done it more than would be normal to do . . .

S: You know that's not true . . . you hardly ever talked to him about your work or the past but since this whole thing started, you've talked to him a lot about how exciting going away to school was for you.

D: I think that's just the age he's got to . . . we go out cycling and so it's hard to talk when we're doing that. I admit I haven't always talked as much to Matthew as I do to Katie because she and I play guitar together and I talk about places I've played music and so on. She asks more . . . I do feel a bit more awkward with Matthew sometimes . . . I've talked to him about this because I do want to prepare him a bit . . .

S: But that's not fair when you know I've been completely against it from the start . . . I told you that he came to me to ask if he *has* to go away to school.

C: How did you answer that?

S: I told him that we were happy with where he was for now and we were discussing future possibilities about education for him and Katie when they change schools at eleven. I told him that we'd obviously talk to both of them about what they want before making any final decision . . . he said, "I know you and dad disagree about this." I told him that we had different points of view and that we needed time to find a way through that . . . just as we do over other things. He hasn't asked again . . . he trusts us to talk to him when the time is right.

D: Shirley's very good when the children ask about things. Of course, it wouldn't be easy for him to go away to school but I know he'd adjust well . . . he's a bright boy.

C: Are you both willing to find out more and discuss at home the alternative options that you've both listed, apart from boarding and the local comprehensive?

S: It would be a relief.

D: I'm willing to do that but I'm not willing to take the boarding option off the table at this point.

C: Okay, I trust both of you to be able to discuss the other options at home. I wonder though if, before we finish this session, you might take a few minutes to say to each other anything that you've either left unsaid or anything that you feel hasn't been heard regarding this issue. It might be helpful again if you can stay with the formula you were using so successfully in the other sessions. *I feel . . . about . . . my idea/fantasy/perception is that . . . What I need for myself is . . . What do you think?*

S: I think that's a good idea.

D: I agree, I think that may be easier here.

C: Okay, who's willing to begin?

D: I don't mind going first.

C: Is that okay with you Shirley?

Shirley nods.

C: It is important that you say this directly to each other.

D: Alright . . . what I haven't said . . . or what I feel hasn't been heard. Well, I feel angry that you've rejected my authority and my opinion as a father and yes, as a man, despite the fact that I've experienced this education myself. My concern is that me being a product of this system isn't good enough for you . . . this has pushed me away and what I need is to feel trusted and respected by you.

S: I'm sorry that you're angry and that you feel rejected . . . It's true that I am rejecting a part of you. When we met I loved your Englishness, your politeness . . . that you were a real gentleman. You were different from a lot of the men I'd met and been out with. You were also like dad, bright, ambitious, and kind . . . but that politeness grew into a cold indifference and lack of intimacy at times of conflict or difficulty. Your, knowing your own mind became arrogance sometimes. I've loved you through that even though it's been difficult for us to talk about things . . . just as you've loved me when I've been too involved with the family, angry about things, argumentative, and stubborn . . . I just can't bear the thought of affectionate, bubbly, spontaneous Matthew having to become "the little English gentleman" and shut down that lovely part of him in order to conform to some "group norm" that takes him far away from us . . . as far away as you go.

D: In that brutal honestly which I love and hate about you, we keep coming back to the same thing that I need to face up to . . . yes, I know I disappear from all of you sometimes . . . I've explained it to myself as, "a man needing to be on his own sometimes" . . . my father was like that and in all honestly, my mother too. One of the reasons that I married you was that you're different from them. You are so open and real and you have a way of responding to people, to children . . . to me. I admire that you know how to put words together and say things, like now . . . I opt out and leave it to you, with the children, with friends, and with family when something "emotional" comes up. I admit that I withdraw, don't know how to deal with that kind of thing . . . I've always thought that we complement each other.

S: I think we do . . . I don't expect us to be the same but the way you are sometimes has too high a cost . . . for you and for me . . . and for the children. I can see these traits in your parents too, much as I care about them, but I don't want this for Matthew and Katie.

D: I need to think about what you've said. I won't just deny it this time.

S: Okay.

I address Shirley.

C: What else might you need to say to David?

S: There's something else I feel you deny and ignore . . . I believe that sometimes, not all the time, you're jealous of my relationship with the children and my family but most of all I think that you're jealous of my relationship with Matthew . . . when he was born, you wouldn't talk about it . . . I think it's natural after us having five years on our own as a couple. I think you find it hard to admit to because Adam was so jealous of you and you don't take it out on anyone the way he did . . . but I wonder if that is sometimes why you withdraw into yourself. My fantasy is that part of the reason you want Matthew to go away to school, unconsciously, is because of that jealousy.

D: . . . that's preposterous . . . ridiculous.

C: Such feelings are fairly common, David.

D: Okay . . . I admit sometimes I do have those feelings . . . I notice that you get on more easily with Matthew than I do. I find Katie much easier and maybe there's a special bond between us just as there is between you and Matthew.

C: That sounds pretty normal to me David.

D: I need time to think about whether it's more than that. I know you've said this before Shirley and I just deny it. I don't really think about that kind of thing. I just accept things as they are. There is some truth in the fact that I don't find it as easy to be with Matthew and sometimes I think he'd get better contact with older men at the school . . . I didn't have a lot of contact with my own father so maybe I'm a bit aware of not being such a good father to him as I am to Katie.

S: Wouldn't he be better off to have more contact with you rather than a teacher or better still both. You're very good with the children when you make the time to be with them . . . Also, we haven't done as much as a family in the last few months because of this problem.

D: I suppose I think I'm being a good father paying for them to have the best education and maybe it is so important to me because I lack confidence in myself as a father, especially with Matthew, at times I don't quite know what to say to him. I don't have your ease with the children . . . I'm more comfortable with the animals.

There is a warmth and honesty about David that has us both smiling.

C: Our time is almost up for today. Is there anything else either of you need to say to each other or to me?

D: I want to have more time with you Shirley as a couple . . . I miss that and sometimes there are so many other people involved in our lives . . . I just want more of you for myself.

S: I miss having fun with you David and especially these past months . . . I can get too immersed in things, family, work . . . it seems to be a vicious circle . . . I've felt lonely and filled my life with other people but the person I most want to do things with is you.

C: Well, over the week, would you discuss those options on your lists and continue to find something to do that you can enjoy together . . . if your relationship is going well then that benefits the whole family as you then have more energy.

We cannot meet the following week so we make an appointment for two weeks ahead. I notice that as they walk down the hallway, David takes Shirley's hand.

Fourth session of counselling

I collect David and Shirley from the waiting room. David is carrying a file. We chat on the way to my room but I feel a tension around them. They sit in their usual seats.

C: So, how would you like to use today?

D: Well, we've had two weeks to discuss the various options that came up last time. It hasn't been easy. We've got a bit polarised in our views again . . .

S: No David, you've hung on tight to your old school as the only real option. So, all the work we've done here, and the research, and reading that I've done has been for nothing . . .

C: So tell me what your thinking is now.

D: I've been willing to look at the other options we discussed last time but I do feel strongly about Matthew following my family tradition and being offered the opportunity to go to my old school. I want to ask him what he thinks about that first . . .

S: . . . and because he wants to please you, he'll agree . . . that's not on. We must have one or two options to put to him that we agree on . . . it isn't fair to offer him a choice that is totally against what I believe in . . . or anything that is totally against what you believe in . . . surely you can see that.

D: I appreciate what you're saying but I know how I feel . . .

S: What is going to happen to us as a family then?

D: To be honest . . . I don't know.

C: Well, this disagreement is very entrenched and in order to focus on what might be behind that, I'd like to suggest that you do a role play of presenting the two main arguments, for and against David's school, but from your partner's perspective. What do you think about doing that?

D: If you think that would be useful.

S: That sounds a bit odd.

I suggest to them that they change seats to do this. They look a bit puzzled but get up and swop over.

C: Okay, so to do this, I want you, David, to put yourself entirely in Shirley's position and present to us the argument *against* your old school. Equally, I want you Shirley to put yourself entirely in David's position and present to us the argument *for* that school. I want you to give your-selves a few moments to think about what your arguments are as the *other* person, but also how you would be feeling in your body, heart, and head. You know each other very well. I want you to really imagine yourself into being each other for this role play.

S: This sounds difficult.

D: I'm not sure I can do this.

C: I just want you to do this the best that you can. It's not only about listen-ing to each other. I want you to get in touch with how the other person really feels, physically, mentally, and emotionally as much as you can. Are you willing to give this a try?

They both nod. I give them a few moments to get into their new role.

D as S: . . . I can picture Matthew being dropped off at the school for the first time by both of us . . . I imagine myself crying and being upset at the first time of leaving him there and us driving away . . . I can imagine the sadness of leaving him there, fear of the unknown . . . I can feel this in my stomach and actually it makes me feel nauseous . . . that's amazing, I can feel it physically . . . Is that how you feel Shirley at the thought of leaving him there?

S: Yes, it is.

D as S: . . . when I think of him walking down those familiar corridors in his uniform, not running and buzzing around as he does at home, I feel sad . . . He used to say to us, "I've got to run," and he would . . . he's

irrepressible in the classroom sometimes and he makes his teachers laugh
. . . things just bubble up inside him . . .

David has tears in his eyes, looks pale and shocked.

> D: I have a memory . . . an old dream I used to have . . . my mother drives
> up to the school at night and knocks loudly on the big double doors shout-
> ing that she's come to collect David Robertson . . . it's time for him to go
> home . . .

David wipes a few tears away with the back of his hand and quickly
recovers.

> D: I'd forgotten that . . . I know I missed my mother, those first few weeks
> . . . I didn't know why I wasn't going home at the weekends as they told
> me I would . . . I think it was different from then on with her . . . I was
> scared to disappoint her . . . I wanted to please her . . . maybe I want to do
> this to please them still . . . I've had a steady "drip drip" of comments from
> Adam about . . . "don't let Shirley stop you from doing what you know is
> right" . . . he's been pushing me for months about all this . . . at any oppor-
> tunity he makes a comment about me allowing myself to be "hen pecked",
> telling me how well Gareth and Edward are doing there . . . asking when
> I'm going to "come to my senses" . . . "there isn't a better place" . . . how
> our parents expect me to "be a man about it all" . . . texting me to "stop
> being a coward" . . . "man up" . . . on and on.

> S: Why haven't you told me any of this?

David puts his head in his hands and holds his forehead as if it could
explode.

> D: I've been ashamed . . . like I was when I was a child and didn't know
> how to stop Adam . . . I've felt humiliated and powerless . . . how could I
> tell you that I've let myself be controlled by him . . . I'm completely
> confused . . . I've got interested in some of the options we've been
> discussing and then I get a comment or text from Adam and I don't know
> what to think any more . . . I feel bullied by him and then I feel I'm bully-
> ing you by not being willing to consider your feelings . . . I'm sorry I
> haven't told you about this.

> S: He's such a bastard . . . I spoke to your mum when we went over there
> last Sunday and she's very open to the other options we've been talking
> about . . . she's pro co-ed schooling . . . she would never put you down like
> that and your dad's much more laid back now he's about to retire, about
> everything . . . this isn't coming from them David . . . you thinking outside

of the box has always threatened Adam . . . like all bullies, he's afraid and hangs on to convention and tradition because he's afraid to think for himself . . . you're not and that's what I've always loved about you.

D: Thank you.

C: It does sound as if there's been another person in the discussion of this issue between the two of you.

S: You're right . . . I can't believe you didn't mention it at all.

D: I'm so sorry Shirley, I think this is a big part of what's made this whole thing so difficult for me and hence for us.

C: Do you think it would be useful for you to talk to your parents, just to get their views, first hand?

D: I will talk to them but I don't need to do that before we make a decision together, just the two of us this time.

C: Okay, I think it's still important to complete Shirley's part of the role play?

S: I'd like to understand more about where David's coming from.

D: I agree.

S as D: Okay . . . well . . . I look back on all the good times I had, when I felt part of something established, safe, trustworthy: I made some important friendships . . . I discovered a talent for numbers which has given me a job I enjoy and a career that connects me with my dad and grandfather . . . all accountants but in completely different areas . . . my mother opened the door to music for me but my school opened my heart to the passion of playing music with other people, singing, writing music, listening to music . . . our art teacher opened up a world of colour, textures, the meaning, creativity, and history of art and how it changes our perception . . . I want Matthew and Katie to have their own experience of that journey of discovery, to have teachers of excellence that equally open up the world to them so that they're inspired . . .

David sits looking amazed.

D: How do you manage to see inside me so . . .

S: I've heard you talk about these things and I know how much your school meant to you but you see, you've already talked about some of these things to Matthew and Katie as well as to me and you have opened up their world and my world . . . they don't need to go to that school . . .

they have you . . . I see you teaching Katie on the guitar and how absorbed you both are . . . I see you helping Matthew with his maths homework and he loves figures as much as you.

David and Shirley both look a bit red eyed.

C: I'd like both of you to move back to the seats that you normally sit in and de-role completely by just taking in the colour and shape of something concrete in this room to ground you both here as yourself. Then perhaps you can talk a bit about how this has been for you both.

D: Well, it's been painful, but amazing to hear Shirley "role play" me . . . You've always *got* me . . . and I've been so immoveable . . . maybe the children can learn from us . . . I think that's been part of my fear, that I wasn't good enough as a father . . . didn't know how to do it . . . I think maybe I'm ready to seriously consider the other options we've been discussing.

S: That would be fantastic . . . I think you *got* me too . . . that physical connection I have to being a mum . . . the loss I would feel . . . in my body . . . I'm a very physical person and it's great that you understand that. I want our children to have good teachers too . . . I want them to experience the best they can but I'm not prepared to pay the price that your mum did and that you did.

C: How is it for you both to realise that you are able to "get each other"?

S: I feel a wave of relief and I know I'm smiling.

C: Yes, you are.

D: I feel a sense of "letting go" of something I've been holding on to uncomfortably tightly and that feels good.

C: What do you think that you are "letting go" of David?

D: Fear . . . that there's only one "right" way ahead for me to be a good father and a good son. There might be another way forward. I won't lose anything by discussing other options and I can trust Shirley and myself to work this out as we have worked out other things.

C: That sounds like an important fear to let go of.

D: Yes, I can see that now.

C: What is your relief about Shirley?

S: I have my David back . . . you always understood me David . . . before this.

D: I may not be fully there yet Shirley but if we talk about it, I might be able to catch up eventually.

C: Is it too soon to take some time to discuss the options from last time?

D: Before my attitude shut down all discussions, we were both willing to look at two options in more detail. First, the independent co-ed school in London, which would probably mean a move. Second, the school near the Ashdown forest, not far from Shirley's sister . . . or another school in or around Brighton . . . I'm quite taken with the idea of us opening another office in Brighton. I talked it through in a very vague way with Grant and Will. Will jumped at the opportunity of spending some time working in Brighton and London, even moving out of London further so they're very open . . . the school might be a bit too "alternative" for me but their results look good . . . I did get as far as starting a file.

David taps the file that he had put down on the coffee table between them.

S: We'll want to visit a few schools. We were so stuck that we didn't get very far with that . . . I spoke to mum and Mary and they were quite keen on the idea of moving nearer to Dorothy but the thought of living near the sea created real excitement . . . they've been on the internet looking at houses ever since but I've insisted that it's early days yet.

C: That all sounds very positive . . . did you manage to spend some time together as a couple since we last met?

S: No way were we up to spending time together once we'd reached the same old stalemate . . . but perhaps we will before we next meet.

C: How do you feel about us having one more session left?

S: Depending how this week goes, it feels okay. I think it'll be easier to find a solution with just David and me making the decision.

D: When we came in today, I was thinking that we needed to ask if we could have some more sessions but it feels as if something important has happened . . . it obviously needs time to be assimilated but one more session feels about right and gives us time to do more research. I feel a bit embarrassed about how entrenched I've been. I think it would be useful to talk a bit more about Adam.

C: What would help you to feel more in touch with your own power around Adam?

D: Having Shirley's support. Remembering that Adam has an agenda and isn't above lying to get his own way and to put me down . . . I know it sounds ridiculous but I get mesmerised by him sometimes and forget what he's like . . . I think, maybe it'll be different each time, but of course it never is.

C: I have a suggestion that some people find useful . . . you could keep a small piece of paper in your pocket with Shirley's name on it. If Adam contacts you, just touch it and allow yourself to feel the power of her support.

D: That's a good idea.

S: I find it hard to be civil to him as it is, this makes it worse but I like Gareth and Edward and I feel a bit sorry for Melanie, who is quiet around him . . . she chats and is friendly enough when he's out of the way.

C: My experience of people that behave as a bully is that deep down they're often very frightened themselves and some of them have no idea that they are bullying other people because they don't have much empathy with others. Maybe it would help you to see the part of him that is a little boy who's so scared that he has to control you. I'm not excusing him but I can't think that it brings him much joy and the fact that he's got away with it for years probably makes him even more afraid. If you can see him as small as he's making himself then maybe he won't frighten you David. I worked with someone once and when they were in their "bullying mode", it helped me to see them as a very comical brightly coloured parrot, pecking away at me . . . it helped to diminish their power rather than lose my own.

D: I rather like that idea . . . I think I'd see Adam as the snake, Kaa, in *Jungle Book*, singing, "Trust in me". He has a way of pulling me in first before he spits his venomous comments at me . . . It's sad really . . . I'd love to be able to talk to him about it. I tried once over lunch when I was a student and all that happened was that I realised that he was in complete denial . . . he doesn't see it . . . I need to accept that I can love him without trusting him . . . I need my guard up . . . and Shirley's name in my pocket.

David smiles at me and at Shirley.

D: I need to keep myself safe and realise it isn't only me he bullies . . . he's been like it with boys at school, fellow students, and I suspect occasionally he's lost good staff because of this.

S: Thank goodness, he isn't our dentist.

D: Weirdly, I've heard he's very kind to his patients . . .

David smiles at Shirley

> *D*: . . . maybe being a bully was *his* coping strategy at school!

> *S*: Maybe it was David.

> *C*: Well, it's nearly time to end. Do either of you have anything else?

> *D*: Only that we will do something good for ourselves this week . . . I think I owe you a meal out Shirley to apologise.

> *S*: I think you do and it'll be expensive . . . I fully admit David that I don't make things easy between us . . . I don't hold back when I'm pissed off with you.

> *D*: But you're honest with me . . . you don't try to control me . . . you usually have good reason to be angry . . . you don't disappear like I do . . . I know where I am with you, even if it's not a good place.

> *C*: I've really enjoyed working with you both today . . . I'm glad you made a break through . . . you deserve to be happy with each other, there's a lot of good will in both of you to make this relationship and your family work well. Enjoy your meal and I look forward to seeing you next week.

We make an appointment for the following week and as I watch them walk down the hallway, David puts his arm round Shirley's shoulder. I am very pleased for them.

Fifth and final counselling session

David and Shirley sit next to each other in the waiting room, both reading. They look peaceful. Once in my room, they settle themselves down in their normal seats.

> *C*: Well, how was your meal?

> *S*: We found a Lebanese restaurant and with the displays of fruit and vegetables, it was like visiting an art gallery of food. I feel as if I have David back from the clutches of his brother and we've been able to talk things through in a very different way. Last week was very helpful and I'm so grateful. I could say that our life seems to have returned to normal but it's more than that. I feel as if we've fast forwarded to a different place and the discussions we're having now are about life style changes for the whole family.

D: It was amazing last time to realise that there were three of us in our discussions and since I've banished Adam from joining in, our discussions have been genuinely productive.

C: How are you dealing with comments from Adam?

D: To be honest, I glance at them and delete them as soon as I see that they're abusive in any way . . . I have a small piece of paper in my pocket with Shirley's name on one side and on the other side her comment from last week that, "I think outside of the box." I was proud of that as I've often seen myself as too "stuffy" and the last person I want to be like is Adam . . . so it helps me to let go of Adam's comment by remembering to touch my connection with Shirley. Thank you for that idea . . . I may have to bring in the "big guns" of the Kaa image next time we make a visit to Adam and his family. I have found though that if I don't react, he eventually stops and changes to someone or something else . . . I think he's picked up my fear and insecurity around this whole issue of schooling for Matthew and that seems to be what he feeds on. I don't want to give the impression that he's always like that. He can be fun to be around but the problem is you don't know when he'll turn . . . like Kaa, you see.

C: Have you got back the intimacy and sexual relationship between you?

S: We have and although it was very tentative initially even that feels different . . . more spontaneous . . . less about "getting it right". This whole thing has cleared a block of some sort. I asked David to tell me when he wants to have space to himself and at least once since last week, he has, and it felt much better than him just "switching off" and me left not knowing why.

D: We've rediscovered having fun and laughing together . . . I feel sad to think how cold I've been this past nine months and I feel bad that I haven't really been able to support Shirley who is obviously still grieving for her dad. We both miss him and so do the children. Shirley had this great idea at the weekend about making a collage of photos of Frank mixed with drawings of him by the children and it's now up on the wall. We all enjoyed putting it together.

S: I haven't felt able to do anything creative, that wasn't to do with work, since he died and although it made me a bit weepy it was a special thing to do.

C: What a wonderful tribute to him.

D: He was very much a family man.

C: So, this is our last meeting together, how do you want to use the rest of this session?

D: I think it would be valuable for us to discuss the main option that seems to have come to the top of the pile. What do you think Shirley?

S: I agree. It's very scary but we're thinking of moving out of London, selling our house in Battersea and moving lock, stock, and barrel to Brighton or on the South Downs . . . somewhere like Lewes . . . It's very early days yet but it feels exciting. We're investigating schools in the Brighton area including the school that started all of this, near to the Ashdown Forest. I'm having to restrain Mum and Mary who already have about fifteen properties they want to look at, all of which overlook the sea in Hove, Brighton, and further along the coast. They've had their two flats valued and realise what they can get for their money and they are completely out of control and geeing each other up into a flat buying frenzy. I've really got my hands full with them and I'm enlisting the help of Dorothy and Pat to calm them down and take it more slowly.

D: They've taken to this whole idea with gusto and we need to think things through at a slower pace . . . it makes sense to make a move at the end of this academic year when Matthew would be changing schools anyway. What's surprised me is the reaction of my colleagues. They're very keen for us to have an office in Brighton as well as the one in London . . . although it's not the best time to expand any business, quite a few of our clients have moved south so it might be good for us.

C: When people make a decision that is good for them, it can often have a positive knock-on effect for the people around them. It's energising to make a big change. How do you both feel about leaving London?

S: It's very scary to think of leaving the only place I've thought of as home . . . especially being a British black woman. London is more multi-cultural. Brighton is a more "white" place to live especially if we live in a smaller town or village . . . that's a bit of an unknown for me. I've only had days out there and don't know it very well. It seems a creative place though and has a buzz of energy that's very like London. I love the Lanes, so many junk shops, book shops, and the café culture is very like London on a smaller scale. There are interesting galleries, theatres, clubs, music, obviously less than London but maybe we'll make more effort to go to what is on. In London, there's so much around all the time that we don't always take advantage of it.

C: It's a big step.

S: Now the real work of decision making.

D: That's what we were talking about on the way here. It's not just about schools now; it's about deciding what life style we want. What location, country or town, different types of school, house, and maybe even a new office. We think we will sell the house in London and rent somewhere for a while and see how the children settle in the schools we choose . . . get a feel for what we really want and what's available.

C: Have you spoken to the children?

S: Yes and they're excited as well but also neither of them want to leave their friends, which is understandable . . . they will only leave London on condition they can come back and visit, which of course they will anyway as Pat and her family are settled firmly in London . . . They'll stay in touch with their friends by email, text, twitter and Facebook, for a while anyway. We want to go and stay down there for a few days in half term to get a feel of the place and visit any of the schools that might be open then . . . luckily they seem to have a different half term so we should see them in action.

D: We're not looking for a boarding school this time.

C: How does that feel for you David?

D: Well, I did speak to both of my parents during the week and they have no agenda at all about where the children go, they just want them and us to be happy . . . they've changed as they've got older. It felt good to talk it through with them. I feel that I have their blessing to do whatever Shirley and I choose, and the children . . . that is a real freedom for me. I've completely let go of my old school as an option, the pressure of that has just disappeared.

C: It sounds as if you thought it was something you ought to do . . . the "right" thing to do to please your parents or Adam but not necessarily something you wanted yourself. What do you think?

D: I think I've been altogether too hung up on a fantasy of being the *perfect* father and *perfect* son.

C: Welcome to the rest of the human race . . . these pressures are all too common.

Shirley turns to David.

S: I do think your "stiff upper lip" comes with an expectation of being *perfect* and I prefer you to be *real*.

D: Thank you, I think that's a compliment.

S: It is. I'm always relieved when you admit to being *human* and *vulnerable*, it makes me feel better about my own weaknesses and mistakes . . .

C: This whole issue has given you both a lot of opportunity for growth hasn't it?

S: It really has. The discussions we've had this week have been as a family and it feels as if we've come through a lot to get to this place.

D: We need a lot more information but staying in Brighton for a few days will give us much more idea and it feels good to be visiting different schools with the children. We're looking for a co-ed, maybe an independent school, and maybe a state school depending on class sizes and we're looking at a couple of alternative schools as well which seem to place a higher value on creativity.

C: It sounds exciting, as if you are throwing everything up in the air and seeing where it lands but within safe guidelines. What sounds good is that you are both being flexible.

D: It does feel as if you've helped us to dig ourselves out of a very large hole that we couldn't see a way out of.

S: A deep hole that didn't seem to have any way out except to break up the family.

C: I'm pretty sure you weren't willing to have that happen or you wouldn't have chosen to come for counselling. I believe that clients who choose counselling are 50% of the way towards resolving their difficulties when they walk in the door, after all it's not easy to ask for help is it?

D: I think the hardest thing for me was admitting that we needed help . . . I wouldn't accept that we couldn't sort it out and that led to us blaming each other for that. I don't know if I would have had the courage to pick up the phone and make an appointment. I did leave that to Shirley. I think I justified that by telling myself, it was her fault so she should find a counsellor. I thought you'd sort her out and it would all be okay. She'd come round to my way of thinking . . . I'm ashamed to think now how arrogant I was.

C: I think it's more likely that you were afraid and didn't know how to get out of a really difficult situation. Scratch the surface of arrogance and mostly underneath you find fear and confusion. Why should we think we have to solve everything on our own when there is help available?

S: It helps me working with little ones because I see that the way they learn is by making the same mistakes again and again until they don't . . . we're the same aren't we . . . just older.

C: How true . . . all my counselling training and yet my best teachers have certainly been my children . . . and my partner . . . they still are.

D: Well that makes me feel better.

We all laugh.

C: You've both worked hard at being prepared to share your feelings here, some of which were very uncomfortable . . . I admire the way you've worked. At the beginning, I wasn't sure which way it was going to go. I'm very pleased that you've found a way of saving and developing a relationship that sounds as if it's strong and has been built on a lot of mutual respect over the years.

D: I think I understand more about why we chose each other in the first place. It's not just coincidence is it?

C: No, I don't think it's quite as random as it seems . . . I know many years ago I read about a psychological experiment about how people choose each other. The researchers invited people to a cocktail party kind of situation. I think there were equal numbers of men and women. It was a limited experiment specifically about heterosexual relationships. The participants were asked to choose a partner they were attracted to and then they looked at what they had in common. Then they were asked to choose another couple and again asked to find out what the two couples had in common. There were too many matches in the experiences of the two individuals and in the two couples for it to be deemed to be merely coincidental. I can't remember much more than that, but from my own experiences of working with couples there is usually both a positive and a negative fit between partners, whether heterosexual or homosexual. The positive fit means it's easier to understand and communicate with each other but the negative fit means that you are often presented with the one person who pushes your buttons and forces you to work through what you most need to change to free yourself of negative or outdated patterns of survival. So in a way both things are valuable but only one may feel like it.

S: That makes sense to me . . . I think the hardest bit for me in this past year has been that I lost your friendship David . . . I stopped trusting you and really didn't know how to get it back. We'd stopped trusting each other and it's hard to love someone when the trust has gone. In this process, I've begun to understand why that happened. That trust still needs to be built up again, I'm wary about what decisions we come to but I do feel as if some huge block has been released.

D: I felt as if the colour went out of my life when we weren't talking and that I lost my best friend . . . I don't want that to ever happen again . . . it's made me appreciate what we do have . . . I agree that it will take time to build up that trust and ease that we had before . . . I'm a bit afraid of what happens if we get stuck again, could we come back for some more counselling?

C: Of course you can, but I believe you'll be fine . . . You've worked hard at being honest and open and at really listening to each other and that is something you won't "unlearn", but yes, if other issues come up, I would be happy to work with you.

D: Thank you, that's reassuring.

C: Is there anything else that you want to talk about before we end?

S: Oh yes . . . I must tell you that out of our discussions this week, although we decided against spending time living in Trinidad, we've decided to have a family holiday there in the summer. We're going with mum and Mary and they can show us where they grew up and there are still some cousins living there to visit . . . I'm really excited. I don't know why I've not even thought of going before but now it seems an important thing to do for me and for the children . . .

D: . . . and for me too. I want to know more about that part of Shirley, it is after all a part of who I fell in love with. I'm looking forward to going . . . who knows we may decide we want to go for longer after all.

S: As I never thought I'd ever live anywhere other than London, just contemplating a move opens up all kinds of possibilities . . . I was as stuck as David in wanting everything to stay the same.

C: Well, I wish you all the very best wherever you decide to be, I've really enjoyed getting to know you both.

D: I've appreciated the space and time you've given us to find our way through what seemed impossible when we first sat here. Thank you.

Shirley reaches down into her bag and brings out a card and a beautifully wrapped bottle and hands it to me.

S: We want you to have this as a thank you for all you've done . . . without your help, I think our family could be in a very different place. I hope we don't have to see you again, if you know what I mean.

We all laugh and I open the lovely card which Shirley has drawn, showing a picture of Brighton pier and the sea lapping on to a beach with six deck chairs on it, one for each of their family plus two older figures looking very excited. The bottle is a very good bottle of red wine.

> C: What a lovely card, I will treasure that . . . and a lovely wine. Thank you very much. With this positive decision of moving to Brighton, it seems like the beginning of a new chapter of your life together, and as a family.

> S: I've got to find a way to calm Mum and Mary down, they could buy anything at the moment . . . luckily we're going to stay in Brighton just the four of us first of all . . . then I may go down and enlist Dorothy's help to look at places with Mum and Mary.

It is natural for us to hug each other as they leave and I find myself with a large smile on my face as they walk off down the hallway.

Michael's story: finding the joy

Reactive (exogenous) depression

There are many different types of depression. At one end of the continuum is a serious clinical depression or endogenous depression, which can be extremely debilitating, including marked psychotic symptoms and will certainly necessitate seeing a doctor, psychotherapist, or psychiatrist who will very likely prescribe antidepressants or antipsychotic drugs to balance the body chemically. At the other end of the continuum would be a less severe reactive depression or exogenous depression which can be a result of a substantial loss or disappointment. This could include the loss of a loved one or other important losses such as: a divorce or separation from a partner; moving away from friends or family; loss of identity, country or place; loss of a job or a chosen career; loss of job security or stress at work; loss of money or good health; social isolation; seasonal adjustment disorder; and even that sense of "emptiness" caused by the absence of "good enough" loving, secure and safe support that children ideally need in their early lives. Within this continuum there are other forms of depression: the depressive phase of manic-depressive or bi-polar illness; involutional melancholia, occurring at the involution period of life (fifty to sixty-five years), very common at menopause (female) and retirement (male); an existential crisis, a crisis of meaning in life, where there can be a general sense of "emptiness" and a response to frustrated aggression. Depression can also be a response to other forms of stress or trauma. It may be accompanied by: feelings of anxiety; loss of motivation and interest; lack of concentration; insomnia; lack of libido; loss of weight; feelings of despair and hopelessness, and depression can be serious enough to tip over into suicidal ideation.

Being depressed is very distressing, especially if we don't know why. Such feelings can be overwhelming and it might be that we find ourselves responding, as a defence or coping strategy by denying or hiding such feelings, sometimes for years. If we are later in a position of strength and balance in our lives, it can be confusing for us to suddenly be beset by depression that does not seem at all relevant to our current situation. This can be a positive opportunity to uncover and integrate dormant feelings that may have remained unacknowledged and unexpressed. It can also be an inner cry for help pushing us to change something important in our lives. Depression can be a result of us having depressed or repressed particular feelings that we need to take ownership of and express. Also, it can be a result of a need to break out from some form of oppression in our lives. Talking therapies can help us to become more emotionally self-aware and emotionally intelligent. There is a dignity in knowing our true feelings and it can also help us to choose what we want to be, to do, or to have in our lives.

Half-hour initial assessment

Michael is shown into my room by our receptionist. I warmly welcome him and shake his hand which feels damp and light in my hand. He gives me his completed top sheet and I notice that he does not make eye contact as I invite him to take a seat. He is white and tall with straight, brown, uneven hair and rather sad eyes. He is wearing smart casual clothes in black and grey that looked large on him. He looks as if he is in his early twenties. He slumps himself down in the chair opposite me. His arms and hands hang over the arms of the chair and he looks at the floor.

C: Thank you for completing the top sheet Michael, it looks as if we have all your contact details and availability and I see that you've signed our confidentiality guidelines. Did you have any questions about them?

M: No.

C: As you probably know already, this is a half-hour assessment for me to find out a bit about you and whether the kind of counselling we offer is appropriate for you; also it gives you an opportunity to ask any questions you may have about counselling so that you can decide if you want to continue to have regular sessions. If you do, it might be me that you see or it might be with another counsellor. Each of those sessions would be for fifty minutes and it's usually weekly for up to a maximum of five sessions."

Michael looks at me a little but mostly he continues to look at the floor. He's very pale.

C: So, I'll be asking you a few things and writing brief notes on this assessment sheet. First, Michael what is it that has particularly caused you to seek counselling now?

M: My doctor told me to come and see someone because of how I was feeling . . . he's given me some antidepressants as well . . . I went to see him because I've lost concentration at work . . . as if I'm going through the motions . . . even when I'm with my girlfriend . . . She's getting fed up with me. It was her who suggested I go and see my doctor . . .

Michael looks up but his shoulders continue to be hunched over.

C: How long have you been feeling like this?

Michael looks out of the window for a while.

M: . . . Hard to say . . . it feels as if I've been in a kind of fog for a long time . . . getting slowly darker . . . not really knowing how to snap out of it . . . I know I'm being a bit unsociable in my house . . . my girlfriend's busy writing up her PhD thesis . . . and I've been sitting in my room too much . . . I feel as if I've less and less energy to do anything outside of work . . . and even at work I feel as if I'm not getting anywhere . . . everything seems to be taking longer . . .

Michael has a soft voice with a slight Lancashire/Welsh accent. When he talks he's hesitant and then just runs out of energy, rather than stops.

C: Can you tell me a bit about your family history?

M: Well . . . I grew up just outside Chester . . . in the same house . . . my dad's got his own law practice there. Mum's a head teacher in a primary school near where we live . . . I've got a younger sister, Kerry, she's seventeen and still at school . . . Mum grew up on a farm in North Wales and moved to Chester when she was a teenager but dad grew up there . . .

Again, he is hesitant and looks down at the floor a lot of the time.

C: What worked well for you in your family relationships and what was more difficult?

M: Well . . . Mum and I, we share a lot of interests and she's very easy going. My dad's more work minded and there's quite a lot of pressure from him to do well and . . . mmm . . . follow in his footsteps really . . .

Michael looks tense and sad. I glance at his top sheet and notice that he is only twenty-three, he seems older.

C: How about Kerry?

M: She's grown up a lot since I've left home and we get on okay now . . . I suppose I thought of her as just a horse-mad kid before . . . she comes down to London and stays sometimes and we're getting to know each other again, which is good . . .

C: Any other family around as you were growing up?

M: My mum's family weren't far away . . . Her dad died when she was a teenager and her mum sold the farm and moved to the Chester area . . . I'm very close to one of my uncles and my aunt and we saw a lot of our gran and the cousins . . . My other uncle went to New Zealand and has a farm there, I spent a gap year after A-levels staying there and working on the farm . . .

C: Did you enjoy it?

M: I did . . . I learnt a lot about sheep.

It is the first time I see Michael smile.

C: What about your dad's family?

M: His parents divorced when I was quite young. My grandmother moved to London and remarried when I was twelve. I see her a little and we get on okay. My grandfather remarried a very nice woman when I about seven or eight and I saw more of them. He was very active in local politics in Chester but died in a car accident a few years ago, when I was twenty ... I was a bit in awe of him but he helped me financially to get through university. He was a very kind man ...

C: What was that like for you losing your grandfather suddenly? Were you able to grieve his loss?

M: It shook me to be honest ... he was a real support to all of us. I know my dad was very upset ... I felt badly being away at university in London ... I came back for the funeral but I couldn't stay long. I really miss him ...

Michael's eyes fill with tears as he talks about his grandfather.

M: He was always there and it was very sudden ... he was a big man and left a big space behind ... if you know what I mean ... my dad still seems a bit lost without him ... perhaps I feel a bit like that too. I think I wasn't able to give proper time to grieving. I wanted to support my dad ...

C: Would it be useful for you to talk to any of your family about him and share with them how much you miss him.

M: I think it would ... I feel quite choked up talking about him ... I feel bad that I haven't seen his wife, Jean, for a while. I miss her as well ... I think it would help me to go and see her next time I'm in Chester.

C: Is there anything else you'd like us to know about your family history?

M: ... Only ... well ... my mum's dad committed suicide after his farm got into financial problems ...

C: I think that's important for us to know ... any history of suicide is important ... have you had any thoughts about suicide yourself?

Michael looks embarrassed.

M: ... That's one of the reasons why I went to see the doctor ... I've had several occasions recently, while driving on motorways ... when I've imagined myself driving into a lorry ... I don't think I'd do it ... I couldn't do that to mum or Kerry but sometimes ... it does feel like a way out of this black hole I seem to have got myself into ...

C: I wonder what it's like when you are in that black hole?

M: ... I can't see a way out ... I feel as if I've been buried alive and no-one can hear me.

C: What a horrible way to feel. I'm glad that you've sought out help because that shows a commitment to yourself to make a change.

M: I feel ashamed that I've let it get this bad . . . that I've even considered suicide.

C: I'm sure there are good reasons as to why you feel the way you do. Also, there's a large gap between having these thoughts, which I think many people have, and actually doing something about it. You've realised that this is a sign, especially in view of your family history, that you need help and you've done something about it by seeing your doctor and coming here. I'm happy to make an appointment in the next week or two to work with you rather than you going on the waiting list. I don't want you to stay with these feelings any longer than you have to. You said that you've been given antidepressants, have you begun to take them?

M: Yes, I saw the doctor four days ago and began taking them the next day . . . I can't say yet that I feel any different . . .

C: I'm sure the doctor explained that it will take a while for them to take effect. Did you tell the doctor about your suicidal thoughts?

M: Yes, I did . . . that's when he suggested the pills . . .

C: Good, you've done well to get help and make sure that you don't have to deal with these feelings and thoughts all by yourself.

Michael makes a small smile.

C: Is it okay with you if we go back to completing the assessment form?

M: Yes, that's fine.

C: Could you tell me a bit about your relationship history? You told me you have a girlfriend, how long have you been together and any other longish term relationships?

M: Gina and I have been together for nearly two years, we were friends before that. At university I had a fairly serious relationship for just over a year and went out with a girl from school back in Chester for a couple of years . . .

C: Do you live with Gina?

M: No, I'm living in a shared house with three friends who I was at college with. Jake and I have been living together for more than three years; the other two have been in the house for nearly two years. It's a good set up and we rub along together pretty well most of the time . . .

C: What is your cultural, ethnic, religious history?

M: Well . . . I'm British and my mum grew up a bit "chapel" in North Wales and my dad was C of E, in name only . . . Mum encouraged us to go to the Sunday School and she'd occasionally go to the local church in our village but we didn't carry on with it once we got to senior school and nor did she really. It's more a social centre in the village . . .

C: Are you on any other medication or seeing the doctor for anything else?

M: No.

C: Have you had any previous counselling or psychiatric support at school, university, anywhere?

M: No.

C: Any other symptoms?

M: Well . . . some anxiety . . . shaking really. It's made me feel less like going out and doing things . . .

C: How long have you been feeling anxious?

M: It's hard to say, it's kind of crept up on me since I've been feeling down . . .

C: What seems to make you most anxious?

M: I've become less confident at work if I have to give presentations and I get a bit afraid of being shaky which makes me more nervous . . . it's mainly in new situations . . . if I'm being appraised . . . I suppose I feel a bit . . . out of control . . .

C: Any other changes, symptoms, or other relevant illnesses?

M: No, I can't think of anything . . .

C: What would you like to achieve from counselling Michael?

M: I just want to clear this fog away and get back to . . . being the old me . . . clear headed and well . . . happy . . . I have so much in my life to feel happy about but . . .

C: Can you think of a time when you last remember feeling happy?

M: Not since I was a student . . . when I met Gina I was working part-time at London Zoo where she's studying . . .

C: Do you enjoy your work now?

M: I've always been reasonably good at it and I was fortunate to get a good placement to do my articles . . . the senior partner is a family friend and we do interesting work . . .

C: I'm not hearing whether you enjoy it or not.

Michael looks out of the window and I realise that his eyes are filling up with tears as he is struggling to answer.

M: . . . I'm sorry . . . I . . .

I point to the tissue box beside him as tears spill down his cheeks.

M: . . . I'm sorry . . .

C: You never have to apologise for having feelings Michael.

M: . . . I . . . just think I've made a big mistake . . . a big mistake . . .

Michael wipes his eyes and takes more tissues. He looks sad and lost.

M: I've spent six years studying law and I can do it well enough . . . sometimes I even enjoy it but . . . most of the time I'm bored to death by it . . .

C: Have you thought about other options, other kinds of work you could do?

M: I know my dad expects me to go back to settle in Chester and work with him, take over the firm one day.

C: And what do you want?

M: I honestly don't know . . .

C: What is it like for you not to know what you want?

M: . . . it's like I feel empty . . . and being scared of that I latch on to what's expected . . . because I don't know what else to do . . . then I feel inadequate compared to other people who are ambitious or have a passion . . . I feel lesser somehow . . . and unfulfilled. Does that make sense?

C: It makes perfect sense and it sounds as if that would be a good focus for the counselling. What do you think?

M: I think that would be good.

For the first time Michael sits back in the chair and he lets out quite a big sigh as he throws the bunched up tissues in the waste bin.

C: It's nearly time for us to finish but as we're going to be working together very soon, I'd like to suggest some homework for you to do before our first session. I'd like you to write a list of as many jobs or types of work that you could imagine yourself doing as you can. You could use a newspaper jobs page as a start and just cut out anything that has a positive energy for you;

absolutely anything. Collect them together and jot down any ideas that come to you and before you come to our first appointment make a list. I realise that it's much more complex than that but it will give us a place to begin. What do you think?

M: I think it'll be good for me to . . . do something . . . and see where we go from there. Thank you.

C: I just need to check out a few more questions before we end. You've already told me that you've had some suicidal thoughts and feelings?

M: Yes . . . but I don't believe I would do anything about it.

C: Okay. Have you ever harmed yourself deliberately or accidentally?

M: No.

C: Have you ever experienced bullying?

M: A little bit at the beginning of senior school until I grew taller than the bully.

Michael grins.

C: Have you ever experienced any sexual assault?

M: No.

C: Have you ever abused food, drugs, or alcohol?

M: I went through drinking too much around fifteen to seventeen but honestly I didn't really like the feeling. That stopped when I went out with my first girlfriend and now I can take it or leave it.

C: Thank you Michael, is there anything you'd like to ask me or anything else you'd like me to know about you for now?

M: No, I can't think of anything else.

We fix up a first counselling session for the following week and I shake hands with Michael at the door. He seems a bit taller as he walks off down the corridor. As I complete the Assessment Summary Sheet, I highlight the suicide risk as low to moderate because of his family history but he does seem to have some good support networks in place and I believe him when he says he will not do anything about it. I did not feel it was necessary to make a "no harm contract" with him at this stage. I think what he is describing might be a cry for help to make a major shift in his life, However, I feel concerned enough to take him on myself and not put him on to the small waiting list that we have, especially as on the top sheet he had completed prior to the assessment he had answered the question: "How is the reason you are seeking counselling impacting on your life? Please circle a number from 1 to 10", with an eight, (1 is "not at all" and 10 is "incapacitating").

First session of counselling

I walk down to the waiting room and Michael is standing up looking at the noticeboard. We chat a bit on the way to my room and he sits, looking a bit more comfortable this week. He is again dressed in dark-coloured casual clothes. He makes eye contact but his face looks very tense and pale.

C: How would you like to begin today?

M: You asked me, last week, to think about work options that might appeal to me. I looked in the newspaper. I thought about it. I just go blank . . . I feel totally trapped in . . . someone else's life . . .

Michael shrugs and looks helpless and close to tears.

C: What do you imagine *your* life would look like?

M: Growing up, all I wanted to do, was to work with animals and become a vet. I worked at Chester Zoo whenever I could. My uncle had a job there so I was fortunate to have the opportunity of working there during holidays and at weekends. I failed to get good enough grades in my science subjects to get a place to study veterinary science . . . Then I made the wrong choice . . . I should have re-taken my science "A-levels" . . . I was persuaded to go with my law option. I got the top grade in law . . . My dad really wanted me to do law and my teachers too. Once I began down that road, I just accepted it . . . now I'm stuck . . . it's my own fault . . .

Michael actually wrings his hands and I feel the anguish in him.

C: You sound very hard on yourself. I know that veterinary science is one of the hardest courses to get into . . . even harder than getting into med. school. It must have been a huge disappointment for you not to get a place.

M: It was the worst time ever . . .

C: As it was something you obviously loved and fully expected to do, have you ever grieved for the loss of it?

M: I'm not sure what you mean . . . It was my own choice . . .

C: It sounds as if your choices were limited by your exam results and the pressures to make a decision. You must have been very sad not to have been able to do what you had always wanted to do.

M: Well, I was surprised last week how sad I felt when I talked about it here . . . I've never really allowed myself to go there . . . It's never occurred to me that I could grieve for something like that and yet that's how I've been feeling all week . . . as if there was a large empty space that I've looked into, that I didn't know was there . . . and it hurts like hell.

C: I'm sure that's very painful.

M: If I've thought about it at all, I've felt angry with myself for messing up my life . . . I haven't been able to see a way out of becoming my father . . . I feel awful to complain about that as he has a very successful life, but to me, what I'm doing, it feels . . . empty . . .

C: Tell me a bit about yourself and what you liked about working with animals.

M: Well . . . I grew up with animals being part of my family . . . my mum loves them and we have a real menagerie at home; she's a typical farmer's daughter. We have a house surrounded by several acres in a village, several miles outside of Chester and we've had dogs, cats, guinea pigs, goats, ponies . . . my sister's a keen horse rider. Mum breeds kunekune pigs originally from New Zealand and they're more like pets really, very friendly and soft natured. We had a weird looking cockatoo which was a rescue bird and she was a real character, my friend really. She died after I went off to University . . . Over the years we've had all sorts of rescue animals. My dad pretends to tolerate them but he gets attached to them too . . . Then working at the zoo, I've got to know all kinds . . . it's hard to explain how much they give to you for very little in return . . . I just thought it would always be like that for me . . . of course, it's hard work too, but the rewards are . . . enormous.

C: As you talk about your home and the animals, your eyes shine and you seem to come alive?

Michael bows his head and cries a little. He takes several tissues, desperately wiping away his tears.

M: I'm sorry . . . I'm really sorry . . .

C: It seems that you may have something very important to grieve for.

M: I can see that I've never really acknowledged . . . this emptiness . . . the frustration of not being able to do what I want. I haven't let myself know how I feel . . . I've been busy being angry with myself . . . blaming myself . . .

C: I don't want to move on to a discussion of what you can do next without honouring and acknowledging the sadness of how it really has been for you the last few years.

M: It's weird that I thought it would help me by going to work on my uncle's farm in New Zealand during a gap year . . . and I worked part time at London Zoo while a student . . . it didn't help . . . a part of me felt worse rather than better . . . it kind of rubbed it in . . . what I was missing . . . I felt like an outsider in a world that used to be familiar to me . . .

C: Have you spoken to anyone about how you felt?

M: No . . . I really haven't understood what I've been hiding even from myself . . .

C: Maybe, just for now, you need to allow yourself to feel that . . . maybe now you are allowing yourself to express it, you'll be able to move on and know what you do want to happen next.

We both sit quietly for a few moments.

C: Who amongst your family or friends do you think would most understand how you feel?

M: I know mum gets it . . . I haven't allowed her in . . . I've pushed her away . . . she knows me too well . . . I've been afraid of this . . .

C: Do you think it would help you to talk with her about it?

M: I've even avoided going home as much because that's also part of what I miss . . . it reminds me too much of what I can't have . . . I find it difficult to share my dad's enthusiasm for the law.

C: Is there anyone else you could talk to?

M: Normally, I could maybe talk to Gina but she's writing up her thesis at the moment and I don't want to burden her . . . I think I could maybe talk to my sister Kerry. She loves horses with the same passion that I love animals. She's in the process of choosing which university she's going to and that depends on whether she stays near home so she can still ride or go somewhere else . . . she's grown up a lot and maybe I could talk to her.

C: That sounds good . . . as if she would understand.

M: Yeah.

C: Do you have any male friends you could talk to about how you feel?

M: Maybe my housemate, Jake. He's been through his parents' divorce recently and he's talked about how upset he is . . . especially about losing his home . . . even though he left home a few years ago . . . it's part of the whole change he's found hard to accept . . . I think he'd understand what I'm feeling.

C: How would you feel about talking to Kerry, Jake, and even your mum, this coming week . . . getting them on side to support you through this?

M: I suppose I've been the strong one . . . it doesn't sit easily with me to ask for support.

C: Has it been a positive thing for you to choose to have some counselling?

M: God, yes . . . I had no idea that all this was going to come out . . . but it took me to have suicidal thoughts and feel as if I might lose Gina for me to go to see the doctor . . . I was really scared of what I might do.

C: Do you still feel scared that you could harm yourself?

M: No . . . I understand that I've been squashing all this down for a long time . . . it's beginning to make sense to me.

C: Sometimes when we experience a loss or trauma, it can be a survival response to bury it inside ourselves as deep as we can. Some things are just too painful. Perhaps we even need time to hibernate with or from those feelings for a time. Then, maybe later, if we feel stronger, older, less traumatised, it comes to the surface in some way or another. We have efficient healing systems inside us physically, emotionally, psychologically, even spiritually and we can let ourselves know in a variety of ways when it's time to make a change, or get help, or just let out painful feelings that we've buried.

M: Well . . . despite the discomfort, I'm relieved to have an explanation of what my feelings might be about and it makes sense to me.

C: You've talked about your depression as a black hole. I'd like to invite you to consider it as a tunnel of feelings that hasn't been fully explored. It can be that we walk into the darkness at the entrance to the tunnel but get scared and rush out again rather than push through the pain that might need to be uncovered. We can keep repeating that walk into and out of that denial or numbing out of the pain at the entrance to the tunnel without knowing that if we only risk feeling it, there can be light at the other end. There's a freedom and the growth of self-awareness that comes from fully expressing and honouring our pain.

M: I can see that when I was eighteen or nineteen, I wasn't at all ready to face the massive disappointment that I felt then. I remember being really scared about what was going on . . . there was even a kind of relief at not having to look too closely at my huge failure . . . a relief to take another path as soon as possible so I didn't have to think . . . or feel. I've not really thought about that before . . . but, it was almost a relief to choose law, which I'd always found came easily. I suppose I heard my dad talk about stuff, grew up with the familiarity of it. I can see now that it seemed an easy option for me.

C: Perhaps a sensible option in terms of career prospects too if it was something you felt confident about?

M: I can see that too.

C: Do you think you could stop punishing yourself about the choice you made?

M: There was a lot I didn't realise at the time . . . I wanted a quick way out and there was a pressure to find a solution.

C: So can you forgive yourself for that now?

M: I have been very angry with myself haven't I?

C: It sounds like it.

M: I don't really know how to let go of that anger and frustration.

C: I have a suggestion.

M: Okay.

C: As homework from today, perhaps you could find a photograph of you at that age, or just imagine yourself as you were then and write a letter to that part of you to tell him that you fully understand how he felt and that you forgive him.

M: It sounds a bit odd but I'm willing to give it a go . . . I know I hated myself for being a failure and letting myself down by not studying harder for what I wanted to do.

C: Were you working at the zoo as well as studying for your exams?

M: I was . . . I assumed that all the practical experience I had would help me to get into vet college . . . I was probably doing too much and I can see that went against me, having less time for my academic work, but I loved it . . . I don't regret the work I was doing.

C: It sounds as if you were doing your best and that's all we can expect of ourselves isn't it?

M: Yes . . . I see that . . . I think I betrayed myself by turning my back on the possibility of a repeat year. I'd already organised things to go to New Zealand and that was a fantastic experience too . . . maybe the choices I made weren't all bad.

C: So maybe all this is what you need to think about as you write your letter.

M: Okay . . . I'll do that.

C: I have another suggestion to go hand in hand with that letter . . . I think it might be helpful for you to write down what you miss about working with animals; what you feel about working in the law firm. Before we even attempt to look for solutions this time, I think it's important for you to explore what you feel about where you have been and where you are now. What do you think?

M: I can see that I need to do it differently this time.

C: I believe it's valuable for you to acknowledge this process of bereavement.

M: Is it about feeling worse in order to feel better?

C: I think it is.

M: Okay, it makes sense to me.

C: You may prefer to draw a picture of yourself, how you felt at that time, how you feel now, and even a picture of how you want to be, past, present, and future. Sometimes it can be useful to draw rather than write things down, or both. It's entirely up to you, how you best do this. I've just made a suggestion based on what some other people have found useful. What I believe is most important is what we talked about earlier, that you talk to others about how you've been feeling.

M: I'll talk to Jake this week and Kerry when I'm home next.

C: When it comes to feelings, I've learnt that anger usually needs expressing, safely; fear is often a sign that we need to protect ourselves; guilt can be valuable for a short time, to learn from, but then we need to think about how long we want to hold on to it before we let it go; happiness is great to share with others, and as for sadness, we need comfort from people who are happy to support us. Any positive way you can find to comfort yourself during this process would be helpful. Some people derive comfort from music, good food, hot baths, a foot or body massage, a walk in beautiful surroundings . . . whatever it is that comforts you, think about doing something nourishing for yourself this week.

M: That sounds good . . .

C: It's a process of letting go, which can clear a path for us to change direction . . . a new beginning.

M: I think that's why I couldn't even begin to consider options for alternative types of work this week. I felt like there was a mountain blocking my ability to think . . . focus . . . experience energy about anything. It's the same thing that's been totally blocking me at work. I used to get excitement from looking at a new case . . . thinking about strategies . . . finding solutions . . . pulling apart the opposition's argument. In the past six months or so it's been like wading through drying concrete . . . the worst bit was not being able to see what I could do about it . . .

Michael's face looks very tense as he is talking about this and I notice that he is wringing his hands again.

C: That can be a very scary place to be.

M: I think that's what's led to me beginning to consider suicide as a possible way out . . . I know that sounds rather dramatic and I hate myself for that too but when I've felt so utterly hopeless, it becomes an option that I think about . . .

C: You told me that your mum's father committed suicide. What do you know about that?

M: Mum was a teenager and she knew the farm was failing financially, even in those days the supermarkets were forcing farmers to lower prices of milk and then, despite all precautions, his herd got sick. It got too much. He didn't know anything other than farming and the farm had been in the family for several generations. He was electrocuted and officially it was an accident but the family, and others, knew it was suicide. There was insurance that could have saved the farm but Gran hated the farm and what it'd done to them so she sold it anyway. She'd always done the farm paperwork so she got a job as a school secretary in a local school just outside Chester and moved the family there. She still lives near to us. I think mum saw him as a bit of a hero, saving the family in the only way he could, but Gran stayed angry with him. They never talk about it with each other as it causes arguments . . . My uncle, Graham, was the eldest son and he was very upset about moving from the farm, that had been the passion of his life . . . as soon as he could, he emigrated to New Zealand and has built up a really successful farm there . . . that's been another cause of anger for my Gran . . .

C: What a hard thing for everyone to face . . . a terrible choice by your Grandfather . . . interesting that your uncle found a way to get back to a way of life that was important to him?

M: Yes . . . I haven't thought about that.

C: Maybe he'd be another person who would really understand how you've felt.

M: He was very supportive when I spent my gap year with him and his family but I hadn't thought about what it would have been like for him losing the farm.

C: Well, it's nearly time for us to finish so let's make an appointment for next week . . . There are a couple of things we've talked about that you could do which may be helpful. Is there anything you want to ask about before we end today's session?

M: No, there's a lot for me to think about . . .

We make an appointment for the following week and Michael looks thoughtful as he walks out of the door. I add a few relevant notes to his family history.

Second session of counselling

Michael smiles up at me from his seat in the waiting room and we chat a bit on the way to my office. He sits down and puts a small zip document case down on the floor beside him.

C: So how would you like to use today Michael?

M: Well, this time I did do some homework. It was difficult to start . . . that's an understatement . . . so many distractions came to mind instead . . . it was the hardest piece of work for me to get going on that I've ever done . . .

Michael reaches down for his document case and takes out a folder which he places on his lap.

M: I couldn't find words at all . . . I spent ages looking at a blank page . . . I couldn't write to the younger me until I drew him and then I did write a letter to him once I'd finished the drawings but I'd like to show these to you first of all. I'm no artist . . . but as soon as I assembled an assortment of old felt tip pens and coloured pencils . . . these three pictures just flew onto the page . . . I didn't write the bit about what I feel I'm missing about not working with animals because in the end, it all seems to be there in the drawings . . .

I clear the coffee table between us and make space for him to lay out the three pictures.

C: So, tell me what you feel about them and what they represent to you.

M: Well . . . really they're self-explanatory . . .

Michael lays out three drawings on the coffee table so that we can both see them clearly. They are labelled: "Then", "Now" and "If only".

M: Well, you can see this is clearly labelled, "Then" and represents how I felt when I got my A-level results and realised that the only two offers I'd received for vet colleges, both conditional on the best possible results, were completely off the table . . . I was devastated and numb with sadness at the time so I've drawn myself with my head bowed in shame and tears making a pool on the floor but they were tears that I never did shed at the time . . . I've drawn a box around myself and that's really where the sadness stayed . . . in a box . . . until coming here. I drew this bubble coming out of my head, containing what had been my dream, and placed it outside of the box . . . This is me working in a laboratory with a test tube and Bunsen burner, working with all kinds of zoo animals, a lion, snake, penguin, chimp; animals I knew from my work at Chester Zoo . . . I'd wanted to work with the animals directly but also saw myself doing research.

C: That's a clear picture and such a pool of tears.

M: I felt sad and tearful as I was drawing it . . . there was no hesitation . . . I knew how I'd felt but at the time I remember being completely numb . . . as if part of me had died . . .

We both stay silent for a few minutes, maybe to honour that young man and his loss and Michael's eyes fill up.

M: Perhaps now is a good time to show you the letter I wrote to him . . .

C: Do you want to maybe imagine placing him in the empty chair over there and read it to him?

M: Well, as it felt a bit weird to write to him at all, I may as well . . . it was much easier to write it once I'd drawn him and saw just how sad he was . . . I was . . .

I move the empty chair a bit forward from the wall so that it directly faces Michael. He reaches into his document case and brings out a white envelope. He opens it up and takes out the letter.

C: Would it help you if I place this first drawing on the empty seat?

M: Yes, I think it would.

C: To help you really imagine him sitting there, could you tell me what he'd be wearing.

M: He'd be wearing jeans and a black T-shirt and trainers.

C: What way would he be sitting? What would his facial expression and hair be like?

M: He'd be sitting on the edge of his seat, anxious to be out of this room. He has his hair longish, just over his collar, with a side parting. He pushes his hair back from his face and has a bit of acne. He looks a bit scared and awkward.

C: He's all yours now.

M: Okay . . .

Michael looks down at the letter, looks at the seat and clears his throat.

M: Well . . . I've written you a letter and I want to read it to you . . .

Hi Mikey,

I've drawn a picture of you. I can see how sad you were and I know how disappointed you were in yourself. I want to tell you that you must forgive yourself for failing to get top grades for your "A-levels" and getting into vet college. I forgive you completely.

You did your best and you were very busy at that time working, revising, having a life with friends when you could . . . there was a lot going on. The colleges raised their academic levels and didn't take account of all the practical experience that you had. If it was going to be *that* academic maybe it wasn't right for you anyway. You would still have been studying and getting more and more into science, which you never loved as much as the animals.

You chose to have a really good time in New Zealand with Uncle Graham and learnt lots of skills and connected with that part of our family. That was important to do, maybe more important.

I'm now getting help to find out what to do next and something good could come out of all of this. So I want you to forgive yourself so that I can live my life now—free of all of that. You weren't a bad person. I'm not a bad person. Sometimes making mistakes helps us do something better. That's what I want to do now. So please forgive yourself so that I can forgive myself now.

Love, Michael

Michael and I stay quiet for a few moments. It feels powerful.

M: Well . . . that was strong . . . I feel for him as well as for me . . . It's weird to talk to a part of you that is past but still kind of there . . .

Michael points to his heart.

C: I believe that every part of us is still there inside of us somewhere, as a memory, as a help to us accessing our child-like excitement and wonder but sometimes as a limitation on our ability to be in the moment because of learnt patterns or even inherited family patterns of responses to painful events and experiences. So, sometimes it can be invaluable to go back and resolve them.

M: I can really see that and I do feel . . . a relief . . . a peace in doing this . . . a kind of softness with myself.

C: Well, when we first talked you were pretty hard on yourself.

M: I was . . . I've felt blocked from being able to give myself a chance to make different choices.

C: Well, that's a giant piece of learning you've done.

M: I suppose it is.

C: I was touched by what you said in your letter. Well done.

M: Thank you.

C: Do you prefer the name Mikey?

M: No, my family call me Mikey still sometimes but when I went to university I preferred to use Michael. It sounded more grown up and I've got used to it.

C: Do you feel ready to go back to the drawings now?

M: Yes, I do.

I push back the chair and replace the drawing on the coffee table with the others.

C: So, what about the second one, you've labelled it "Now"?

M: Well, it's crammed full . . . again rather self-explanatory . . . there's me tightly dressed up in my work suit, shirt, and tie standing by my desk, lap-top, a huge pile of papers on the desk, law books on the shelves, and surprise surprise . . . the box has become a cage . . . no animals in sight . . . I've become the exhibit in a different type of zoo.

C: Is that how you feel about your job?

M: I certainly feel as if I have to perform . . . that I'm on show . . . tightly dressed . . . as soon as I get home I have to take off my work clothes and put on more comfortable clothes.

C: I've thought they almost seem too large for you.

M: Have you . . . well, maybe I buy them loose to counteract feeling so tightly held in by my suit . . .

C: You're smiling in the picture.

M: Yes, that's the fixed smile, tight like everything else . . . it doesn't feel real . . . I hate it all really . . . drawing this made me realise just how much . . . sometimes I pace up and down the office and feel just like a lion in the zoo or the circus . . . maybe more appropriate.

Michael shakes his head from side to side and he looks both hurt and angry at the same time.

C: When you look at this picture, how do you feel?

M: Trapped . . . above all . . . trapped . . . It looks bizarre to see myself in the very cage I've chosen to put myself in . . . no-one else has put me there and I'm the only one with the key . . . I don't think I realised that I felt so strongly about it . . . I thought it would get better and there are aspects of my job that I really enjoy . . . that looking for creative solutions . . . but most of all, I'm surrounded by tons of reference books, hours on the internet, and miles and miles of paper . . . that really is what my desk looks like, piles and piles of papers . . . books piled up around my desk . . . no room to move . . .

C: When I look at this picture, I feel disturbed by your confinement in that tight suit and in that confined space. It feels as if there's no room for manoeuvre. It's certainly not a place you'd be able to stay for very long.

M: . . . I have to find a way out . . . a positive way out . . . I know that won't be easy . . . but it's crazy to stay in a world where I feel like that . . . maybe I've worked in zoos for too long to recognise how uncomfortable a cage really is.

C: So what about your third drawing?

M: Well, that came so easily . . . as soon as I began to draw I knew I needed to be free . . . to be outside . . . I must find work that enables me to spend time in the fresh air, in nature, exploring . . . maybe some form of conservation work . . . I know I would enjoy working with animals in their natural habitat. The hills in the background represented a landscape somewhere in Africa, hence the elephant . . . the tent represents freedom and the desire to explore . . . the people around the campfire could have been young people and may represent some form of teaching. It's strange that when you asked me to write what I might want to do, words just don't come . . . as soon as I began to draw . . . images jumped into my mind of possibilities.

C: I notice you are wearing a T-shirt and shorts in the picture.

Michael grins widely.

M: Yes, and a pair of comfortable trainers.

C: How do you feel when you look at this picture?

M: As if I can breathe, my arms are out, my legs apart . . . everything about me in this picture is open to the elements . . . my smile is less "painted on" and more genuine . . . I haven't let myself even imagine a future like this . . . but I know this has much of what I want and need in my life . . . I have no idea how I can achieve this or even if it's possible . . . but now I've seen myself in this open place . . . how can I stay confined?

C: I see you've titled the picture, "If only", what do you think needs to happen to make this a real possibility rather than an "if only"?

M: Well, a cage confines but it can become a comfortable place to be . . . even the wildest animals after years of being in a zoo find it impossible to exist in the wild, they've lost the ability to fend for themselves . . . I've accepted a financially comfortable way of life . . . a secure future in our family law firm waits for me once I've qualified . . . I would cause a lot of pain and hurt to my father in particular if I decide to opt out. If I return to studies or retrain, I wouldn't be in a position to set up home with Gina for years, if that's what we decide to do . . . there's a lot to think about . . . before I can decide what I want I have to consider very seriously what I would be letting go of . . .

C: I think that's very wise of you and all of those things need thinking about . . . perhaps there are ways of combining your present career and a future that is more about animals and conservation . . . you have qualifications you can build on . . . skills that are transferable skills and lots of practical experiences from your zoo work.

M: How can I know what is truly right for me?

C: What some people have found useful is to write a list of options and make a list of pros and cons for each option and choose a score of ten for each pro and each con . . . include any and every option you can think of. What do you think?

M: That sounds like a good idea.

C: Before you begin, it would be very useful for you to get more information, either by talking to someone in a Career's Office or looking up courses on animals, conservation, conservation law, and any other area or organisation that you can find out about. Could you go back and use the Career's Office of your university or law school?

M: Yes, I could do it on-line or call in one lunch time, I'm not too far away . . . that's a really good idea . . . as I said before, I've been too blocked to even consider doing that before and now . . . I think it's time . . . I feel an excitement to do this.

C: That's great . . . did you talk to anyone this past week? You mentioned talking to Jake.

M: I told him I was having some counselling because I'd been feeling down . . . of course he was aware of that but I'd not got into any conversations with him about it before . . . it was helpful to be able to talk to him a bit . . . it turns out that he'd had some counselling during his sixth form when a good friend of his died in a motorbike accident. It was good to talk with him and, of course, he understood why I feel the way I do. We didn't have long as we were both busy this week but it opened a door to being able to talk more in future . . . Kerry's coming down to stay this weekend, so I might talk to her as well.

C: From your time in New Zealand, do you think farming is something you'd consider?

M: No, I thoroughly enjoyed it but it did put me off a bit . . . it was sheep, sheep, and more sheep . . . not that kind of farming anyway . . . I did e-mail my uncle Graham yesterday and said a bit about wanting to make a change but not sure what yet . . . I didn't mention the counselling but I did tell him, I wasn't happy doing the work I'm doing . . . I haven't heard anything back yet.

C: Well, it's nearly time to finish and it feels as if you've achieved a lot today. Did you feel it was useful to do the drawings?

M: I thought it was a bit odd at first but I'm amazed how easy it was and each picture gave me a real insight . . . I would do it again, if I wanted to know about how I was feeling . . . sometimes, I think our heads, even words, can get in the way . . . this seemed to be a way of by-passing that . . . very useful.

C: So, let's make an appointment for next time and I wish you luck with your research.

As it turns out Michael is away for a couple of days the following week so we make an appointment for two weeks ahead. As he walks off down the corridor I feel as if there is a real shift going on for him.

Third session of counselling

On my way down to the waiting room, I find Michael walking up and down in the corridor carrying his small document case. He smiles and looks energised and I notice he is wearing a bright green jumper, the first time I've seen him wearing something colourful.

C: It's two weeks since we met last, so how would you like to use this session?

M: I feel as if I've made some real progress in this past two weeks. I've researched all kinds of different possibilities but most important of all, I feel a change in myself . . . a determination to make a real change. My sister, Kerry came to stay with me, just after the last session and I took her out for a meal specifically to talk about coming here and what's been going on for me. She couldn't have been more supportive and I was surprised how much that helped.

C: It's great that you've given her a chance to support you.

M: Yes . . . that's true and it's helped to create a stronger and very positive relationship between us . . . we talked about all sorts of things. She has lots of questions about what she wants to do too. She's studying English and history as her main subjects but is actually doing particularly well this year in law, which she took as an added extra. She's always wanted to go to university but probably work with horses but she's think-ing that next year she may apply to do law instead. How weird is that?

C: She's at that time of change for everyone and, as you well know, it's really difficult to make firm decisions about your whole future then. In the present financial climate and precarious job market, people may change direction several times. How would you feel if Kerry studied law and worked in your father's firm?

M: My immediate reaction is relief . . . that I'd been let off the hook . . . but I wouldn't want her to feel the pressure to do that because of me. I told her that too. She laughed at me and asked if I'd ever known her do anything she really didn't want to do and truly I haven't. She's quite a free spirit . . . if she found she still wanted to work with horses or do anything else, she'd make it happen.

C: So what about you? What can you make happen?

Michael takes out a few sheets of paper from his document case.

M: I looked at job pages and marked jobs that appealed to me and wrote a list of some of those; I looked on the internet at courses to do with those jobs and to do with conservation and phoned a few people. I found some very interesting courses at the University of Kent that I didn't know about. It shows how blocked I was after my A-level results . . . I've been completely blinkered about other possibilities. I can really understand what you were saying about that tunnel of pain . . . I can't believe how much that prevented me from seeing what was out there . . .

C: Sometimes, it's easier to avoid the pain but you seem to no longer be doing that?

M: It does feel as if I'm really beginning to move through the tunnel so that I can see there is light at the other end. Even during my years as a law student, when I was doing casual work at London Zoo . . . there were people I could have talked to about other options but I was on one track . . . the only track I allowed myself to consider . . . there really was a brick wall in the way . . . no . . . a huge mountain . . . it was as if the rest of the world was shut off for me . . . I enjoyed talking to Gina about her course at UCL and her research at the zoo but it was a door that I'd completely closed for myself.

C: Feelings of loss, failure, guilt, frustration, and the sheer heaviness of grief can do that.

M: This process has been extremely humbling and painful for me, coming here, and although I am beginning to see a way through it . . . there is something else . . .

Michael's voice slightly cracked and he looked sad.

M: I had a long talk with Gina this weekend and even though she's incredibly stressed, writing up her thesis. She was very honest and admitted that she'd stopped seeing our relationship as having a future but hasn't really had the time or energy to think about it or talk to me . . . I feel very stupid that I hadn't really seen this coming and realise I could lose a relationship that's very important to me.

C: I'm sorry about that. Do you want to take some time today to talk about this?

M: Yes, I do . . . I suppose I'm afraid that she's lost respect for me. I haven't been much fun to be around since I got further and further into this job and most important of all . . . I haven't been giving her the support she needs at this difficult time . . .

C: It seems to me that you are both doing very stressful things at the same time, which puts any relationship under enormous pressure.

M: Gina feels as if she's been carrying me emotionally for some time and that's been too much . . . she's right . . . I don't think I saw it, but now I do . . . she's glad that I'm coming here but . . . maybe it's too late for us.

C: How do you feel about that?

M: I think if it'd happened before I came here, I might have used it as an excuse to end everything . . .

C: Do you mean that you might have committed suicide?

M: The way I was thinking and feeling then, I think this would have been one step too far for me to imagine that I could survive . . . so yes, I'm afraid of what I might have done then . . . but I don't feel like that anymore . . .

C: What's made that difference?

M: I've begun to believe in myself, that I can make things happen that enable me to live the way I want to . . . I've thought about the fact that if I make the changes I need to make and depending where she gets a job after her PhD . . . we could be living far apart anyway . . .

C: These days, many couples are forced to make difficult decisions about accepting jobs that mean living far away from each other.

M: What's changed for me is that before going through this process, I know I'd have tried to hang on to Gina, no matter what . . . and I don't want to do that. She's very important to me and I hope we can work something out . . . but if I lose her now, it isn't the end of my world . . . it isn't sitting on top of that mountain of loss that I came here with . . . I don't want to carry on with a relationship that we're not both committed to . . .

C: This sounds like a big change for you Michael.

M: It is . . .

C: It was good that Gina could talk to you about this?

M: Yes . . . she admitted that she wasn't sure if she feels this way because she's pressurised at the moment but she wants us to cool it for a bit . . . I realise that it might not work for us to go back to being friends but we agreed to see how that goes until she finishes her thesis . . . also, I think I really need to sort myself out and decide what I'm going to do. Obviously, I hope that we can work it out but I know I can cope even if we end up going our separate ways . . . I don't feel so afraid of everything.

C: What do you think has made you less afraid?

M: I don't feel stuck in one groove any more . . . I honestly didn't believe that I could have what I wanted or make things happen for myself . . . in coming here . . . I realise I don't have to do it all on my own . . . even talking to Kerry. She's really there for me . . . and I didn't mention that I had a long e-mail back from my Uncle Graham. He wrote a bit about what it'd been like for him when he lost all prospects of working on the farm, something he'd just taken for granted as he grew up . . . he'd been devastated by his dad's death . . . and he also lost a way of life that he loved . . . he'd felt very down, confused, and rejected for a long time. It was a really supportive e-mail. We got on well when I spent my gap year there . . . I don't keep in touch as much as I'd like to, so I ended up phoning him and we talked for quite a while . . . I didn't realise before it was him who'd found my grandfather after he'd killed himself. He told me that he'd been very angry when he ran away to New Zealand. It'd been a long struggle for him but after years of working for other people, he saved enough to buy his own farm. I know it helped that he married a farmer's daughter and now he has a huge farm . . . I talked over a few ideas with him and he was encouraging.

C: Has it made you consider working with him again as a possible option?

M: No . . . I enjoyed my time working on the farm but it's not a life that appeals to me. I enjoyed the whole experience and the time I spent with Graham and his family but I like living here in the UK . . . I do have a hankering to go and work in an African country . . . that wildness stirs something in me . . . I feel like that about the animals I've worked with who belong out in the wild.

C: So is this a good point to return to talking about the options you've been looking at this week?

M: Okay . . . well, I found some interesting MSc courses that I could just about afford to do full-time for a year. My grandfather left me some money which has helped me through college and there's a little left that I was going to use as a deposit for a house, eventually. I could just about manage if I got some part-time work as well . . . There's an MSc in Conservation Science, which I did know about, at Imperial College, and I'm meeting up with a friend of Gina's who did that one . . . I've also arranged to go and talk to someone down at Canterbury in Kent where there's an interesting looking MSc, a taught course in Conservation Project Management and another one in Conservation and Biodiversity . . . both of those may take some account of the practical experience I've had working with animals and luckily at uni, I did take an optional course on Conservation Law so that would help me a lot . . .

C: That all sounds very interesting.

M: Despite feeling pretty shitty about the situation with Gina, there's a part of me that feels excited . . . as if I might be able to bang on a door that could open for me to a very different life beyond it . . . maybe even the picture I drew , "If only" . . . I hardly dare imagine that I can do this but the last two weeks at work have been so stifling that I thought I might just stop breathing and I have dared to imagine that I could put that behind me.

C: Were there other possibilities that you thought about from the jobs that you looked at?

Michael unfolds the sheets of paper that he's holding. In talking about his job options, his whole energy has shifted, his eyes are alive, and his face animated.

M: I wrote a list of ten options: three were the MSc courses that I've mentioned; three were jobs working with animals, of these two were voluntary internships in zoos, one in the UK and one in France, the other one, working with rescue animals, is so poorly paid that it might just as well be voluntary by the time I paid for accommodation; one was a job with the RSPB on a reserve in Anglesey; two were with animal charities, again one of those was an unpaid internship and the other was temporary, covering maternity leave; the last one was the option of joining a law firm that works in conservation law, once I've finished my articles . . . I asked around and a friend of mine from law school knows a woman who'd worked with this company recently but they're cutting staff at the moment.

C: You've been busy, that's quite an impressive list of work in different areas . . . did you score them?

M: I did but obviously, I need more information . . . I'm meeting a few people in the next couple of weeks: the woman who worked in the law firm, who may know other openings; the friend of Gina's who did the Conservation Science course; I've booked to meet up with someone at the University of Kent to discuss the Conservation courses there.

C: Can you see how much you've developed: the confidence and boldness to risk believing that you can really have what you want; the power to propel yourself out into the world; the courage to risk asserting yourself to make a new positive future happen for yourself. You've been very efficient and effective in banging down that door haven't you?

M: I suppose I have. I feel very different. I've fought for other people in my law work but I feel as if I've found my fight for myself. That does feel good. I've even decided to contact my uncle in Chester who knows some-one who used to run an RSPB reserve . . . that's a big step as I haven't told anyone at home other than Kerry about the fact that I might leave my job.

C: How do you feel about that?

M: As you ask me my stomach tightens and I realise I'm scared.

C: Who or what is scaring you most?

M: Well . . . obviously my dad is the person who will be most disap-pointed and angry with me . . . it is the hardest thing for me to let him down. His father helped him set up his first law practice in Chester . . . it's been assumed that I'll join the firm when I qualify . . . he was pleased that I wanted to learn what I could in London in a larger practice and take that experience home with me. I've always wanted to live back in Chester . . . but I wanted to study and work in London and have different experiences, especially being able work at London Zoo, even part-time . . . dad was so proud and pleased when I decided to study law . . .

C: I understand your fear and your feelings for your dad but, can you take a few moments to reflect on whether you'd rather let yourself down?

Michael looks at me and blows out a deep breath.

M: . . . In some ways I would . . . but I accept that my first responsibility is to live my own life and that's what I'm learning to do . . . sometimes you have to hurt other people in the process and that's not easy. I'm scared of doing that. It would've been easier if I'd got into vet school in the first place. What's hard is that I've given my dad false hope for years.

C: That's hard for both of you. What are you afraid might happen?

M: In a way, it's the unknown that I'm afraid of . . . I have a fantasy that maybe he won't want anything to do with me anymore, that he'll disown me . . .

C: That is quite an extreme reaction . . . could you talk to your mother first?

M: I'd planned to do that . . . I think she'll be pleased for me . . . she's very perceptive and knows me well . . . she's tried to talk to me often over the years . . . asking if I'm really happy . . . I know she sees my pain . . . always has . . .

Michael is tearful again.

M: I've avoided talking to her about it ever since I made the decision to study law. I get a bit gruff with her if she ever brings it up . . . honestly, I think that's partly why I decided to study so far away from home . . . it's weird how well she can read me . . . she'll be pleased for me . . . she loves animals too. My uncle Colin, the one who works at Chester Zoo, says our house is a small zoo . . . I will talk to her first but I know it's time for me to face up to my dad on my own . . . it'll be one of the hardest things I've ever had to do . . . my anxiety will grow the longer I leave it . . . I've already thought I might go home this coming weekend as it's a long weekend and I think I need to talk to him then.

C: That's very brave of you.

M: I don't see myself as brave considering how long I've been on the wrong path . . . too scared to change it.

C: Sometimes we take what seems like an easy option until we realise that it isn't.

M: That's true . . . I can't hide my true feelings from myself anymore.

C: Is there anything else that we might talk about before we end today that would help you to face your dad?

M: I can't think of anything.

C: Would you like to do a role play and put your dad in the empty chair and talk to him here first.

M: It might help . . . okay.

I get up and move the empty chair a bit nearer to Michael and turn it directly towards him. I notice that he tenses up in his seat.

C: Is that too close to you?

M: It feels a bit close but also quite realistic.

C: So as we did before in the previous session when you put your younger self in the empty chair, take some time to really image your dad sitting there . . . tell me what he'd be wearing.

M: Well, I'd wait until he'd changed into his cords, jumper, and casual shoes, so he'd be comfortably dressed, not in his suit, straight from the office.

C: How would he sit and be with you?

M: He'd sit right back in the chair and cross his legs. He'd probably be relaxing with a cup of tea. That always comes first when he gets home from work. He'd be reading the newspaper but if I sat opposite him, he'd put it down and be open to talking.

C: What about you, before you speak to him, can you imagine that place inside you that wants to be true to yourself, a place of strength, knowing, and courage from which you need to speak to your dad?

M: . . . It feels as if I need to speak to him from my heart . . . as I say that, I can feel my heart pumping.

Michael has his arms in his lap and looks very pale but as he speaks about his heart pumping, he puts his forearms on the arms of the chair and that seems to ground him.

C: Okay, so he's all yours.

M: . . . I want to talk to you dad about something that's very important to me. I realise that this might be difficult for you to hear . . . I've been having some counselling for just over a month because, since I began with Thompson, Reeves, & Co, I've become more and more depressed and anxious. My doctor prescribed antidepressants and suggested that I talk to someone . . . the counselling has really helped me to realise that I made a mistake going into the law rather than choosing to find another way of working with animals, after my A-levels. As a result I've decided that I can't finish my Articles and that I need to make a change as soon as I can to a different job or further study that will help me do what I really want to do . . .

Michael stops for a bit.

... I'm sorry because I know that I must be a big disappointment to you and I'm sure you're angry with me, but I can't do this job any more . . . I've looked into other possibilities and I want to use what's left of Grandpa's money to either study or work in some kind of conservation work . . . it might be that I can combine my experience of the law with this work and my degree would certainly help me get onto an MSc programme to pursue some kind of project management in that field . . . I'm looking into lots of possibilities and I wanted to tell you what I've decided to do . . .

C: That sounds really good Michael, how do you feel?

M: I'm nervous and tense but it feels like a relief to say what's really going on for me . . . I can't believe I kept going without saying anything to anyone . . . even myself . . .

C: Would you like to sit in your dad's chair and role play him receiving and replying to what you've said?

M: Okay, I'll see if I can.

Michael goes over to the empty chair and sits right back in the chair and crosses his legs. He takes a few moments to put himself in that place.

M as his D: I'm sorry that you don't want to follow the law Michael because I thought you were happy doing it. You've been very successful in your placement and I've heard good reports about you . . . but I'm sorry that you've been feeling depressed. It sounds as if you've got help and I'm glad for that but I'm really sorry that you've been so unhappy, son, and we haven't been able to help you. You sound as if you've moved forward and know your own mind and what you want to do. I'm genuinely pleased about that. It sounds as if you'll still be able to use your law degree and all your experiences of working with animals as a step into further education. It's your life, son, and I'd not want to pressurise you into something that isn't right for you. I hope you know that . . .

Michael goes back to his chair.

M: Thanks dad, I'm sorry that we won't be working together.

Michael moves back into the empty chair.

M as his D: Me too son, but it doesn't mean we can't still do things together does it?

M: I'm pleased that you've taken this so well.

Michael looks over at me.

C: How did that feel?

M: That was better by far than I'd thought . . . I felt strong and I realised that he would listen and understand when I thought about how he's been about other things . . . I just imagined conversations I've had with him about my exams and when I damaged my first car on a concrete post turning into a car park.

C: It's not as if you want to give up everything. You've come up with some very good ideas, you have a direction that you want to go in . . . you're considering further study which takes you forward successfully to a field you already have a lot of practical experience in.

M: My main worries were about the family thing . . . I know he was looking forward to us building something together . . . he's very proud of what he's built.

C: Is there any chance of practising some kind of Conservation Law work within the firm?

M: It isn't impossible . . . but it's totally not what he's about . . .

C: For now, take one step at a time. No more pressure to do anything that you're not completely committed to . . . It's a big thing to talk to your father . . . a big step.

M: Something else I realised in looking up stuff on the internet was that I still feel strong links to Chester Zoo and they have their own Conservation Programme called, "Act for Wildlife". I've been so switched off from my past self that I haven't followed what they've been doing and there are some projects they're involved in which I wouldn't mind helping with . . . I really need to sit down with my Uncle Colin and find out what's going on there . . . I haven't spoken to him for ages and I know he's heavily involved with the black rhino projects which are the animals he's worked with for years . . . I was doing all sorts at the zoo but for a while I was lucky enough to work with the Nigerian chimps and it sounds as if the zoo is helping with some interesting conservation projects, returning chimps to the wild in Nigeria. Also, I'd like to get involved in teaching the local young people if there was anything I could offer . . . sometimes I used to help teach groups of young teenagers visiting the zoo and I enjoyed that . . . I may take a day or two of holiday and spend a bit longer at home . . . unless it all goes terribly wrong with my dad.

C: It sounds as if you'll be away for our next appointment, would you prefer for us to meet up again in another two weeks?

M: I think it will have to be . . . even though I have some difficult stuff going on with Gina and with my dad . . . I feel today's been really helpful. Also, I'll have had time to find out more information by the time we meet again.

C: Before we end, even though we talked a bit about it earlier, I want to check out with you whether you've had any further thoughts about suicide.

M: I really haven't . . . that seems to have been a huge weight lifted . . . I don't know if that's the result of the antidepressants or just what we've talked about here but as I said earlier even this whole thing with Gina which has made me very sad . . . it feels different . . . more real. I'm able to talk about it with Jake, and one of the other guys in the house, and I'll talk to Kerry when I go home, probably my mum too.

C: I think antidepressants can be a valuable support and especially when taken in conjunction with counselling. You've coped really well with the situation with Gina and I wish you the best of luck in talking to your dad. So, let's make an appointment for two weeks' time.

We set an appointment time and I walk Michael down the corridor as I need to go to the office for something. He does seem much easier with himself, tense and pale but not weighed down in the same way as he was when I first met him.

Fourth session of counselling

Michael looks quite tanned as I greet him in the waiting room. His eyes have more sparkle and I notice that he is again wearing more colour, a deep red shirt. He settles comfortably back in his seat.

C: I imagine it's been a busy and eventful two weeks so what would you like to talk about today?

M: It has indeed, some very difficult parts I'd like to talk about and lots of ideas buzzing around to sort out into some kind of direction . . . I've been looking forward to coming today to do just that . . . not sure where to start . . . maybe with my dad.

C: Okay, good.

Michael sits forward on the edge of his seat and looks nervous.

M: I did go back to Chester for the long weekend break and added a couple of days to talk to my uncle and other people at the zoo, in particular, a woman I worked with about five years ago, who was very helpful . . . anyway . . . I waited for a space to talk to my dad when we wouldn't be interrupted . . . it took until the Sunday afternoon . . . I was nervous . . . but I found that place of strength and courage inside me and spoke from my heart. I was very humbled by the fact that what concerned him most of all was my visit to the doctor, the fact that I was on antidepressants, and how bad I'd felt. He'd no idea that was how I'd been feeling and I suppose he was a bit shocked . . . then I felt guilty that I hadn't been able to talk to him before . . .

C: It sounds as if he cares about you a great deal.

M: I feel bad about not telling him and my mum how I was feeling . . . I'd felt so guilty about letting him down . . . he was obviously disappointed and said he'd been looking forward to us working together, but he's always known how much I loved working with animals . . . he thought I'd just accepted that I couldn't become a vet and moved on. He told me that mum had always questioned whether I was doing the right thing for myself.

C: You were saying last time that your mum had doubts about what you were doing.

M: I spoke to mum the day before, because we'd had lunch together on our own. She wasn't at all surprised by any of it but she was shocked by how bad I'd been feeling. She made me promise that I would always talk to them if I ever felt like that again. She was very upset that I hadn't said anything to anyone in the family or to friends when I'd been feeling so desperate. It frightened her. She promised not to say anything to my dad until I'd had a chance to talk to him myself the following day. They were both pleased that I was coming here. Over the rest of my time at home, I had several conversations with them individually and together. I decided to share the pictures I'd done with them both . . . again they were upset that I could've been feeling so bad and yet didn't feel able to talk to them . . . I explained that I honestly didn't know how much I'd buried and hidden even from myself. I told them about our sessions and some of the things we've talked about . . . that all helped . . . I hadn't thought how bad they'd feel that I hadn't been able to share this with them . . . although I realise that I hurt them both, I think they understood . . . in the end . . .

C: It's a very hard thing to understand how deeply we can bury our feelings sometimes. It was brave of you to share the pictures . . . and to be so open and honest with them.

M: My dad's quite conventional normally but I suppose he's had years of being married to my mum and her family are a little more eccentric . . . he's much more open minded than I thought he would be, considering his background . . . we've all learnt a lot more about each other . . . I don't think I knew just *how* supportive my dad would be . . .

Michael's eyes were welling up with tears. He took a tissue and dabbed them a little.

M: I feel a bit stupid for not realising how much they love me no matter what I do . . .

C: Oh Michael, fear, loss, shame, feelings generally can mix us up and spin us round so that we lose all perspective about ourselves and even about people that we love . . . it sounds as if you've achieved something very important in your relationship with yourself and with your parents.

M: I suppose you're right . . . I do think I've been stuck in the entrance to that tunnel and feel rather stupid that it wasn't as long or dark as it felt while I was going round and round at the entrance . . . that image helps me.

C: I'm so glad for you that you've been able to get through this, but these things are risky and hard to do, hard for them as well . . . I hope you can forgive yourself as we all get it wrong sometimes. Welcome to the rest of the human race!

Michael attempts a grin and relaxes back in his chair again.

M: I won't forget how good it is to get support and not have to do it all on my own . . . I talked more to Kerry as well so we all ended up talking about the options I've been looking into . . . which was helpful, mostly . . . my family can get a bit carried away with ideas sometimes so I did have to reign them in a bit. My dad phoned a few contacts about Conservation Law firms and I've another good contact in London to talk to.

C: It's great to have support from your family.

M: Also, Kerry was able to tell them that she's been thinking about doing law as her main subject next year as she's predicted a good grade in her exams . . . of course, then we all checked out with her that she wasn't responding to any pressure about me opting out of law . . . I don't think that will be allowed to happen again.

C: It sounds as if you've opened the door to more honest communication.

M: I haven't thought of it like that.

C: How was the meeting with your uncle?

M: My head's going round and round a bit with so many ideas and possibilities opening up . . . I'm excited and thoroughly enjoyed my visit to Chester Zoo . . . some of the staff and animals I worked with were still around so it took a while. A woman I knew from before, who works with the Nigerian chimps, has been involved in a very interesting project in Nigeria and there's a chance that I could become a volunteer this summer . . . because of my experience, they may be able to provide some basic accommodation if I pay my own fare out there . . .

C: That sounds very exciting.

M: It really does . . . anyway then I spoke to the course director at the University of Kent about the Conservation MSc courses there and I think that of all the courses in London, and in Canterbury, and two others I've discovered, I'm most interested in the MSc in Conservation and Project Management . . . they'd be willing to consider me because of the practical experience I already have but especially if I work in Nigeria this summer for a few months . . . I can see how I could get back on track doing something I really love that combines working with animals and the law and admin experience that I have . . .

C: That's good news.

Michael pulls out a folded piece of paper from his shirt pocket.

M: I wrote a long list of possibilities, which keeps getting longer. I scored the pros and cons of the top five—out of a possible score of ten—as you'd suggested and the Conservation and Project Management course came up top of the list . . . I applied for a temporary job for a few months with the RSPB which could count as a suitable field project as well but I haven't heard anything yet. I still have a couple of people to talk to about Conservation Law so that option is incomplete. I've sent off applications to a couple of charities including one called Born Free which needs French translators and luckily I did a language course in French at Uni. I'm even looking into the possibilities of working towards a Postgraduate Certificate in Education eventually. I like the idea of teaching about conservation, that came out fourth on my list . . . not sure how I'd fit that in . . . second on my list was the course in Conservation and Biodiversity, and third was surprisingly the idea of going back to do work in the zoo, if I could combine it with project work and teaching . . . the fifth one was the possibility of working in a law firm that was dedicated to protecting conservation projects and areas . . . sorry that must all seem rather muddled . . . would you like to see my list?

C: You have been very busy so yes, I would.

Michael handed me the piece of paper which made everything a lot clearer.

Options for "If only"

1. Conservation and Project Management MSc managing practical projects with some teaching. (10)
2. Conservation and Biodiversity MSc—similar with above plus teaching (9)
3. Zoo work including projects overseas and teaching home and overseas (9)
4. Teaching about conservation in schools, zoos, giving talks, home and overseas (8)
5. Law firm specialising in important conservation protection home and overseas (6)

C: I love your title Michael.

M: Sorry, I'm just so excited and realise how much I have to tell you . . . the other thing is that as soon as I got back from home, I handed in my notice at work . . . that wasn't easy. I've always been someone who sees things through. I normally finish what I start. It's been difficult to opt out of an agreement and I feel bad that I may have taken a place that someone else could have had.

C: It's a place someone else can now have.

M: I suppose so, but I'm afraid I've let down my team and my immediate boss who's been very patient with me these past months.

C: It's more important not to let down yourself. Would you rather carry on, "for them"?

M: No . . . no . . . I know it's the right thing to do, it's been a change for me . . . I've often felt obliged to do things and this whole process has made me really think about what I need to do for myself . . . it feels a bit selfish sometimes, that's all.

C: I went to a talk recently given by a wise teacher and he talked of two types of selfishness, one being negative and one being wise. I think that when you choose to do something that will create happiness for yourself;

that is certainly a "wise selfishness". He also talked about "protecting our enthusiasm" and I must say that as you talk about these ideas, you are alight with an enthusiasm which is a delight to see.

M: Thank you, I feel full of energy . . . a very different feeling from that heaviness I've been carrying for the past few years.

C: I'm thinking that you may not need to have another session Michael. What do you think?

M: I do feel as if I'm on track at the moment and despite facing some diffi-cult situations, I haven't slipped back into that awful place.

C: I agree, I think you moved a mountain and now you're running down the path in front of you.

We both laughed.

C: How would you feel if we end today but that if you feel, at some point, that you'd like another, you can phone and book a "check in" session?

M: That sounds good to me.

C: Is there anything else you'd like to discuss today?

M: My relationship with Gina is something I wanted to talk about . . . We've met up a few times and it's kind of weird . . . now I'm excited about the future . . . Gina seems kind of angry with me . . . I'm not sure why.

C: Is she still writing up her thesis?

M: Yes, but it sounds as if it's going okay . . . I've accepted that, for now, we meet as friends and I've tried to be supportive in practical ways, taking over takeaway meals, doing things for her around the flat so she can focus on work. I was away for four days and she wanted to get on with her writing . . . I don't really understand . . . I'm feeling more upbeat than I've felt for years but whatever I say seems to irritate her.

C: Have you spoken to her about it?

M: I've asked her if she's angry with me and she says that she isn't . . . I even asked her if there is anyone else but she got even angrier with me . . . I feel as if whatever I do is the wrong thing at the moment . . . I understand that I wasn't much fun to be around but I feel that having accepted "just being friends" has made it worse . . .

C: What I know about writing up a PhD thesis is that anxiety levels rise enormously . . . perhaps you need to see how it goes and be patient until she's through this . . . also, although she wanted you to get help, she doesn't know what you might be doing in the next year or two . . . you've changed and whereas you were the reliable, employed, stable person, this is now a time of transition for *both* of you . . . also, maybe she wanted you to "fight" for her a bit.

M: Maybe I've accepted it a bit too easily . . . we're both changing and nothing is as it was . . . I know that Gina's anxious and when I think about it, she's pushed me away before when she was going through a problem with her supervisor . . . I think it's how she deals with stress . . . not so different from what I was doing. I don't want to lose her and maybe my new found confidence and energy is hard for her as well.

C: Even positive change can be stressful, like the preparation for a holiday can be as stressful as a busy time at work.

M: I need to trust that if it's a strong enough relationship, we'll get through this whatever we each decide to do in the next year or two . . . the other thing is that I have more faith in myself that I can cope if we don't . . . when I came here I'd lost that faith.

C: Perhaps this is a good point to review the work we've done together?

M: I came here because the doctor suggested it might help, along with the pills, I have to say I didn't really believe that there was a way out of "the cage".

C: That's a horrible place to be.

M: I don't think I would have taken my life but I was feeling less and less in control and I think the thought of being out of control while I was driving matched exactly how I felt . . . I was moving forward on a path that I didn't want to be on and had no power, no strength, no will or way of knowing how I could stop or turn around or take a different turning . . . I didn't know I could change it and that was unbearable . . .

Michael looks sad.

C: You'd been on that "wrong road" for nearly six years . . . that's a long time to feel trapped or "out of control".

M: Until I talked about it here, I didn't realise that I was actually in pain . . . it was heavy, oppressive and stole my energy, my ability to feel happy, even my ability to love. It felt like a monster had sucked the very life out of me and what was left was that empty black tunnel and no peace, only a trembling need to find my way back to something I'd known but couldn't get in touch with any more.

C: You describe it very well.

M: I've had time to think about it and what I've learnt here is that I can change, but I don't have to do it on my own . . . seeking support, finding support really helped me . . . going to the doctor, talking to you here, talking to Jake, Kerry, Gina, both uncles, and my parents . . . why didn't I know that I could do that . . . they've always been there for me?

C: Pain can paralyse us from taking action, we can all feel crushed by feelings: fear, trauma, anger, guilt, shame, humiliation, grief, sorrow . . . feelings can be overwhelming but you were willing to risk getting help and then you were willing to use it well.

M: I think that having sought help once, if I was in that position again I hope I would do the same.

C: Taking any action can make us feel more powerful . . . I know if I'm feeling nervous about starting something, I can break through that barrier by just tipping out my handbag and clearing it out . . . other people I know clear out files, wash up, clear out their wardrobe, just *to act* can be enough to make it easier to move forward. You were willing to risk being vulnerable.

M: It was surprisingly frightening to ask for help . . . it's never come easy for me to ask for support. My mum and dad are much the same, we're pretty self-sufficient . . . I know I thought I should sort things out myself but had no idea how stuck I was . . . thank you for making the whole thing possible for me.

C: I've really enjoyed seeing your energy come back.

M: While I was at home, I decided to stop taking the antidepressants . . . I've been back to see the doctor and he's okay about it . . . he thinks it has been a "reactive depression" and that the changes I'm making will help enormously . . . I've promised him I'll go back straight away if I have a bad reaction.

C: That's good because you're taking good care of yourself.

M: I don't ever want to get myself into this position again . . . I'd lost myself and was in danger of becoming a replica of my dad and we're very different people.

C: I don't think you will Michael. Don't forget if you want another session, give the service a ring and I'll make myself available . . . I think you're going to be very busy in the next month or two and I wish you all the very best with whatever you decide to do. It's been a real pleasure to work with you.

M: Thank you, if I don't come back, I'll let you know.

C: That would be great.

We take our leave of each other and I feel very proud of Michael as he walks off down the hallway.

*   *   *

A few months later I get an airmail card from him, with a picture of a chimp on the front, which reads:

Dear Maggie,

I had to write to you when I realised that I was standing around the camp here with tents lined up and hills behind us and someone is lighting up a campfire, oh yes, I'm wearing a T-shirt and shorts, no elephant, but otherwise it's just like my "If only" drawing. I'm actually based several miles away but I'm visiting with a group gradually releasing two rescued chimps back out into the wild. I've been accepted on that MSc programme next year and am doing project work for six months here as a volunteer. The main thing is I feel as free as the chimps we're releasing out into the wild. Thank you for showing me where the key was—in my own hand!

Warmest wishes, Michael

Karen's story: finding a reason to live

Addiction and abuse

Addiction can be a desire to numb out from overwhelming or frightening feeling, a need to escape from the pain of living into a perceived sense of unity. It can be a way of self-harming and taken to its extreme, an expression of finding it just too unbearable to live in this world anymore; a slow form of suicide. Both addiction and depression can be masking a deep unacknowledged, unexpressed deprivation, loss, longing, fear, hurt, or anger. In the book *The Continuum Concept*, Jean Liedloff (1989) states:

> Of all the expressions of in-arms deprivation, perhaps research will confirm that one of the most direct is addiction to narcotics like heroin. Only research will be able to ascertain the precise relationship between deprivation and addiction, and when it does, the many forms of addiction—to alcohol, tobacco, gambling, barbiturates or nail biting—may begin to make sense in the light of the continuum concept of human requirements.

She goes on to describe some addicts' experiences and highlights that the heroin experience, in particular, "is like the feeling the infant has in arms". Although heroin addiction is extreme, even lesser drug addictions help to return the addict to a place of infant like self-absorption, dependence, and no responsibility. Her hypothesis was that babies require a large amount of "babes in arm" experience during the first six months of life in order to properly achieve independence. I believe that this may be equally effective from a "mother figure" or "father figure". This important developmental stage requires a sufficiency of secure bodily contact mixed with vital human stimulation, including play.

This need to escape could also go back earlier than this to the blissful state of life in the womb where everything is taken care of, all needs are met, and all responsibility is "suspended". If something happens to shake our faith, trust, or belief that we *deserve to be* and *will* be carried and supported successfully by ourselves, family, friends, and indeed life itself then we may crave sensations that take us back to a simulation of that time of blissful dependence.

Almost anything can be used as a focus of addiction and they can be interchangeable. We live in a society where much money is made from our vulnerability to addiction. In the 1970s, I remember reading in the book by Professor John Yudkin (2012), *Pure White and Deadly*, that he believed that tobacco companies put sugar into the filter tips of cigarettes to make them more addictive, as if nicotine wasn't bad enough.

Common reasons for drug use

It is part of adolescence to experiment with different behaviours including the use of drugs, alcohol, and other potentially harmful behaviours. Some of the reasons for this are:

- A legitimate way of searching for serenity (spirituality) and resting the mind from emotional and mental strain-a quick move to "being" from "doing".
- A legitimate way of reducing physical pain—accepted in some medical circles.
- The release of tension or stress.
- Rebellion—a "rebellious child" response to perceived "critical parent" (terms used in the book by Harris (2012): *I'm Ok, You're Ok*), experienced in childhood at home or at school. A way of then choosing to be out of control.

- A transitional object—a substitute parent or "outer authority" until we find our own "inner authority". It is possible that, for those of us who are most likely to look to an outer authority to define ourselves, it would be easier to be attracted to substance abuse of some kind or another.
- Peer pressure, being afraid of saying no.
- A ritualistic urge or an initiation—ritual is an important part of human life which may have been missing and drug taking may be a way of returning to some missed ritual.
- A search for experience expanded states of consciousness as with LSD, etc.
- The creation of a community and context—a way of making friends and giving a sense of belonging to a "family" who have a shared purpose for coming together—this may be more prevalent for young people who have moved away from home for study or work who might feel a deep social "loss of community". This may also be part of freeing the self from parental values—making a stand with our own generation.
- Curiosity—risk taking—how far can we take it and not get "hooked"—testing ourselves and our body against an opponent.
- Fear of, or resistance to, the responsibility of growing up and taking a full part in mature adult life—wanting to stay adolescent and not wanting to take on responsibility for ourselves, just yet.
- Young people are vulnerable to the mass media culture promoting anything that makes them more "acceptable", "cool", able to achieve perceived "perfection".
- There are the hidden addictive substances added to processed food and drinks such as sugar, fat, and salt on which people can become dependent.

Reasons for moving into drug abuse

A move into longer term dependency or addiction can prevent the growth and development of the individual into the good health, well-being, maturity, and responsibility of adulthood. Some of the reasons for this are:

- A swop from one addiction to another.
- Parental role modelling of addiction.

- A way of maintaining denial of self, the systematic stifling or denying of our needs for self-expression and self-actualisation.
- A way of numbing out from emotional pain and psychological distress. This may inhibit our self-awareness and ability to make healthier choices for ourselves.
- A transitional object which is not easy to let go of—especially if there is an abusive or neglectful parent which may be being manifested in the drug.
- Drugs can enable us to mask our problems and appear to be functioning normally, in the short term.
- A way of self-harming, feeling dissociated or alienated from the self, and not knowing how to nurture the self.
- Slow suicide—a desire to destroy our body. This could stem from an unexpressed desire to destroy an abusive, rejecting, over controlling parent in ourselves. We may be seeing our body as an adversary.
- The repression of our energy, power, or creativity—many of us are afraid of how powerful and amazing we are and how successful we could be. Drugs can become one of many ways to suppress the self.
- Low energy—a desperate search for more energy. We may be prepared to try anything to renew and recharge our energy. It may be that we have not only stopped recognising hunger, fatigue, discomfort, and our needs for rest, caring, or nurturing but we may feel undeserving of these needs.
- A deeper longing for greater contact with life, meaning, purpose—misguided in addiction.
- A transcendence of everyday boredom.
- A way of coping with the challenges of a pressurised working, home, or student life.
- A search for something outside of ourselves to change things rather than implementing inner change.

Sexual abuse from an addicted parent, as presented in this story, would include several of these reasons for moving into drug abuse. When I began counselling, hearing stories of childhood sexual abuse was one of the hardest things to hear and accept about what we humans do to one another. I had no difficulty in believing that such stories were true when there were such similarities in the experiences that clients shared and the effects that it had in those families.

What I find amazing and incredible is how children can not only survive and thrive but can grow into brave, compassionate, joyful, creative, bright, and strong members of our society despite the cruelty that they may experience in their young lives and although some do, the vast majority of survivors do not go on and abuse others.

Having worked with people at a deep level of trust and truth, I have been humbled by the amazing potential within the human spirit. Those human qualities of resilience and fortitude can enable us to overcome almost anything from the past and still form a real trust and optimism about our future.

> Resilience is a sweater knitted from developmental, emotional and social strands of wool. (Boris Cyrulnik, 2009)

Half-hour initial assessment

Karen finally turns up, late, for her assessment after three cancellations. After three such cancellations, our office manager normally asks clients to re-book again in a few months once they were sure they were both willing and able to attend their appointments. Something in Karen's voice had got through to our very experienced office manager and she decides to offer a fourth appointment. I find her intuition in such matters to be extremely perceptive. Karen is given a few minutes to complete the top sheet in the waiting room so I go and collect her there. She is just signing the bottom of the sheet as I go in. I extend a warm welcome to her and shake her hand. She gathers up coat and bag and walks along to my room full of apology about her lateness and the cancellations, talking very fast. She is well dressed, medium height, and slim. She's a white woman, with short blonde hair that frames her face, dark blue eyes, and slightly blotchy skin. She hangs her coat up on the peg by the door in my room and sits down on the edge of her seat.

Karen: I'm really sorry. It's hard for me to get away from work with every-thing going down at the moment.

Counsellor: What is your work?

K: I work as a dealer for a large investment bank and as you can imagine, its fraught with pressure at the moment with the markets being so volatile.

C: I can imagine. Well, let's use the time we have as best we can, we have just over twenty minutes left. I see you've completed the form with all your contact details and availability and I see you've signed the confidentiality guidelines. Do you have any questions about them?

K: No.

C: Today is a prelude to counselling; an opportunity for me to find out a bit about you and assess whether the kind of counselling we offer is appropriate for you; also, it gives you an opportunity to ask any questions you may have about counselling so that you can decide if you want to go on to have regular sessions. If you do, it might be me that you see or another counsellor. Those sessions are usually weekly for fifty minutes up to a maximum of five sessions. There are a number of questions so I'll run through them and see how far we get today, do stop me if you want to ask anything at all.

Karen nods and I notice she is picking at bits of skin on her forehead and in front of her ears. She seems nervous. I smile at her to reassure her.

C: What made you decide to come for counselling at this time Karen?

K: I've thought about it lots of times but I don't really believe anyone else can help. I know I've got to sort myself out. Then, a friend told me how useful she'd found it. I thought I'd give it a go. I don't really know where to begin. What made me pick up the phone was that I really messed up at work a month ago. I don't do that. I can't afford to do that. One more mistake like that and I'll be out. Everyone seems to hate the bankers and we do earn a lot and spend a lot but there's a relentless demand to perform. There's no place for failure. I suppose it's got to me. I don't know if anything or anyone can help me.

C: How long have you been feeling like, "it's got to you"?

K: Maybe the last few months but mostly since I messed up. I put it right . . . this time . . . but it scared me shitless. As long as it all goes okay, it's great. The money's good. I bought my own flat in Docklands five years ago. Have a lot of "things" that I like. No time for a "life" though.

Karen laughs but she is tapping one of her feet on the floor and her whole body seems agitated, still picking at the skin on her face.

K: Work starts early in the morning with breakfast meetings. We're on the go all day, rows of computer screens, pounded by information from all over the globe, keeping up with what's happening, everywhere. Can't miss the tiniest detail, some uprising or rebellion somewhere can have enormous effects on the markets. Have to keep it all in my head. When I get home, late, the news doesn't stop. Don't get me wrong I love dealing. I love figures, how the markets work, finding a way in to make a "killing" that no-one else has seen. Maybe, I've been doing it too long. I know people who get burnt out. I started straight from university. I did computing with maths and got a first. They snapped me up. Now it feels as if they own me.

C: It sounds like a highly pressurised job that you do. Can you tell me a bit about your family history?

K: I don't talk about my father.

Karen looks very tense and tight lipped.

C: It would be helpful for me to have an outline of your background and family relationships if we are to work together but I respect the fact that there may be individuals you don't want to specifically talk about. Could you just tell me if he is still living?

K: My father's dead.

C: How long ago did he die?

K: Five years ago.

Karen looks out of the window, her shoulders hunched, fingers in front of her mouth and looks as if this is all she wants to say about her father for now.

C: Is your mum still alive?

K: Yes, I see her sometimes, she's alright. We get on okay these days but I don't see her at home because my brother's living back there. He's a pain these days, drinks too much. I see his ex. She had the sense to leave him years ago. She's been a friend since we were in infant school together. Only good thing about my brother is Graham, ten and Emily, seven. They're my family now along with their mum, Becks.

C: Do you have any other brothers or sisters, grandparents that you see?

K: No. My father's parents died when I was a teenager, my grandfather was a right bastard. They lived on the same estate we did. Nan was okay but she was bashed around by him and died when I was at Uni. They had a daughter who died when she was little; she was run over. Their other daughter went to live in Australia, probably to escape. Mum's dad died about eight years ago and her mum's in a home in Manchester near my aunt. They used to live in London but my aunt moved away when she got married and my Gran moved up north to be near to her and my cousins after my granddad died. We've never seen much of them 'cos my dad took against my aunt. My Gran's a bit out of it these days. Mum visits her occasionally and now my dad's dead, she's free to stay with my aunt.

C: I need to ask about your relationship history. Are you in a relationship at the moment?

K: No time. I had a relationship at Uni . . . American guy on an exchange programme. He went back to his home university in California. We wrote for a while but it didn't come to anything. Since then, it's been work, occasional dates here and there, nothing serious.

I check her top sheet.

C: You're thirty-four?

K: Yes

C: How would you define your cultural, ethnic, religious history?

K: I'm a Londoner through and through and we never went to church or anything. I don't believe in anything really.

C: Are you seeing your doctor for anything, any medication or illnesses?

K: I never go if I can help it.

C: Have you had any previous counselling or therapy?

K: Never thought of it before. I'm used to relying on myself.

C: What do you want to achieve from counselling?

K: Don't know really. I want to get back to being "on the ball". My head feels as if it could explode. I can't think straight anymore. I've got to get back on track. Can you help me to do that?

C: I can explore with you in these sessions what might be getting in your way and help you find a way through that.

K: Okay.

C: How will you know when you've got where you want to be?

K: I'd feel as if I'm back in the driving seat, going fast but not veering all over the road.

C: What do you think might get in your way of you achieving what you want to achieve?

For the first time, Karen stops and thinks, rather than her quick punchy answers.

K: My past feels a bit like a can of worms that I'm not sure I want to open.

C: A can of worms can be opened a bit at a time but to keep that inside may be getting in your way. I'll leave that for you think about as you're deciding if you want to continue with the counselling.

K: Okay, I know we don't have much time left.

C: Is there anything else you think might be useful for me to know about you or any questions that you want to ask about the counselling?

K: No.

C: I need to finish with some questions about your safety and experiences. Have you ever experienced any suicidal feelings or thoughts?

K: Not for a long time, when I was younger.

C: How old?

K: From eight or nine until I went to senior school.

C: That's very young. I'm sorry that you felt like that. Have you ever harmed yourself accidentally or deliberately?

K: As a teenager I used to cut myself quite a lot but not now.

C: When was the last time you harmed yourself?

K: Probably when I was at university.

C: Have you experienced any bullying?

K: My immediate boss at work is a bully but nothing I can't handle. He takes the credit for the good work I do but lands me in it if I make a mistake. I have my own way of dealing with that. I make sure the right people know. It doesn't bother me that much.

C: Have you experienced any sexual assault?

K: In the past.

I feel a "shut down" in Karen and I decide to hold off on this one, especially as we have little time and I find myself talking a bit faster, which is what Karen is doing too.

C: Have you ever abused food, drugs, or alcohol?

K: All three at different times.

This sounds like throwaway comment.

C: Any of those serious and current?

K: I used to abuse alcohol from about twelve to fourteen and then it started to make me sick. That's when I stopped eating. I suppose I was anorexic up until I left home. I left home at sixteen and I gradually got back to normal eating. Drugs have been more of a problem. I started at around fourteen taking all sorts. I was in a crowd that took drugs rather than alcohol. It's been off and on since then. I still dabble a bit in cocaine. It's prevalent in the world I work in. It keeps us awake and it used to keep me energised and "on the ball".

C: Are you continuing to take it?

K: I suppose it's become a bit of a problem and that may be why I've started to make mistakes. I've got overconfident and maybe it's got a bit out of control. I used to have long periods completely off it. Now, I find that more difficult but I cut down every so often. Since I messed up at work, I've cut down drastically. I'm normally strong and determined with things like that.

C: Have you thought of getting support at a Rehab. Centre, it doesn't have to be residential?

K: I suppose this is my first attempt to "put my toe in the water".

C: I want to support you getting the help that will be most effective for you. What I suggest is that we work together for the five sessions, beginning as soon as you can make the time. How would you feel about that?

K: That sounds okay. I still have doubts whether anyone can help me except myself.

C: It sounds as if you've done a lot for yourself already. You have a home, a successful career, some family that you enjoy being with, and you've taken the risk to come and ask for support. We can discuss your various options in our sessions together. It may be that you will need to consider moving on into some kind of longer term programme of support that includes things like meditation and some kind of body work, as well as therapy and/or group work with specialist drug therapists.

K: I appreciate that.

C: It's been difficult for you to get here for these assessments. Would you normally be able to make this time?

K: I think so and if not, I'll try and let you know as soon as possible. Things do come up at work that I have no control over that require me to take immediate action.

C: Could you find someone who might be prepared to cover for you for these five sessions?

K: I think I could.

C: There needs to be a commitment from you to come to these sessions, for yourself, if this is going to work.

K: I think that's the problem for me, to commit to myself.

C: Also, I want to be sure you are keeping yourself safe. I hear what you say about taking yourself off the cocaine every so often but I'd like to make sure you are safe to do that. I think it's extremely important for you to see your doctor and discuss your options in terms of medical support. Would you be prepared to do that?

K: I get what you're saying. I'll think about that.

C: Good, I think we can work together well. I'm hearing that maybe our focus needs to be about what would enable you to commit to your recovery, initially for the five sessions, but then for longer term support to come off the cocaine completely. What do you think?

K: I think that's probably why I'm here.

C: Then, I look forward to working with you. Shall we make an appointment for next week?

We make the appointment for next week and I walk down the hallway with Karen who chats all the way.

First session of counselling

Karen reschedules the appointment we made three times which means that it is nearly four weeks since we last met. As I greet her in the waiting room, she's very apologetic.

K: I'm so sorry that I've had to change this so many times and twice with only a day's notice.

Karen apologises and explains all the way to my room and hurriedly sits down, again on the edge of her seat.

C: I am concerned about your readiness to do this work. How committed are you to yourself as well as the counselling?

K: I want to do it. I know there's a lot that I've been sitting on for years, especially about my family life. I can see that there are things I'm doing in my life that are self-destructive and I don't want to carry on. I wanted to come back but I'm not sure how it's going to help just talking about it.

C: I can understand how you feel and hear that you want to do it. There's another step that's required and that is having the will to work at this. That begins with the commitment to come to appointments. I have two questions for you: "What do you most need to change?" and "Do you have the will to change it?"

K: Okay. The problem is that what I need to change isn't necessarily what I want to change. I've obviously thought about this a lot. I need to change some of my habits. Some of those habits help me in my work.

C: "What do you think you need to change?" and "What do you think helps you in your work?"

K: I know I take too much cocaine. I'm finding it hard to stay off it. I'm cutting back at the moment to just one or two grams a day, which is a small amount for me. It helps me to feel more confident and helps me to have the energy to work the hours I have to do to be successful.

C: What is true in what you've just said and what is the addiction talking?

K: You don't mince words do you?

C: Not when I'm dealing with a system that needs to be challenged for your good health or even your life. I'm sure we both know what sustained use of cocaine leads to.

K: Okay. I've been an addict and it's now affecting my ability to work effectively.

C: How long have you taken cocaine on a regular basis?

K: At college and university I took quite a lot of dope which continued for a few years afterwards. I took cocaine occasionally, at parties. Then, I'd use it if I had an important job to finish or when I needed to think more clearly. It gave me the energy and confidence if I had to give a presentation or had to get up early after a late night. Fortunately, I couldn't afford to take it regularly and my first priority was always to buy a home of my own. I got this job about five years ago and bought my flat. Rather than making me feel more secure, I felt afraid. I was scared that I could lose my home if I lost my job. I couldn't bear that. Lots of people I knew were made redundant over that period. About four years ago I began to take cocaine regularly to keep the highs; the confidence; the energy going. I couldn't cope with the depression, the deep tiredness of coming down. I was able to keep it to about three grams a day and come off it at weekends if I slept a lot. This past year, it's gradually crept up to four or five grams daily and less weekends without it. I usually inject it. I've honestly believed I had it under control until this big mistake a couple of months ago. I managed to cover my tracks but it was a fluke that I got through it. I was so close to losing it all.

As Karen talks about this, she is picking at the skin on her forehead, in front of her ears, and on her forearms. She has one leg crossed over the other and her foot is in constant movement.

C: Have you attempted to come off drugs completely?

K: Not very successfully. I know I talk myself back into it again. I'm good at conning myself.

C: So, would you still say, "I used to be an addict"?

K: Okay . . . I am a cocaine addict.

C: How do you deal with the withdrawal symptoms of reducing it?

K: I've taken your advice and went to the doctors. I got a young woman doctor who I could talk to and it was her who suggested that I continue to cut down rather than attempt to abstain as yet. She gave me some sleeping pills and suggested some auricular acupuncture. I've been twice and I can't say it's been that helpful yet but I've been able to stay with using only about two grams a day. So far, since coming here, it hasn't crept up. She was glad I was talking to someone and she agreed with you that it would be good to seek some longer term help in a Rehab. Centre. She was very blunt and told me that I needed to know that cocaine destroys talent as well as lives and that whatever I might be afraid of, it would get worse on cocaine. That was a bit of a wake-up call. She's also booked me in for all kinds of tests and I'll see her again when all the results are back. Again, I've had to postpone some of them.

C: I'm so glad you went to see your GP and it sounds as if you are tackling this in a much more realistic way. I hope you will re-schedule the tests; that's important. Well done.

K: I've been going to the gym and running regularly to deal with the extreme anxiety and it all helps a bit but mainly, I can't make these mistakes any more. I don't have a choice if I want to keep my job and that's my life.

C: Have you ever talked to anyone before about being addicted to cocaine?

K: No-one professional. My sister-in-law, Becks, who's known me forever, she knows and used to take a variety of drugs years ago. Other people have probably guessed, especially other colleagues using, but I've never told anyone else before; maybe not even myself.

C: Then you've already begun the process of recovery.

K: Maybe.

Karen stops picking at the skin on her forehead and stops moving her foot. She is noticeably still for the first time in our sessions and looks thoughtful.

C: As regards this counselling Karen, some clients successfully use brief counselling, rather like a kindergarten, as a step into longer term therapy. I'd like to support you to understand how you've come to this place and to strengthen that will of yours to commit to the process. We have a list of Rehab. Centres in London that we would recommend. What do you think?

K: I'll think about it and see how this goes first.

C: Good, let's move away from the cocaine now. I'd like you to tell me more about you and how you began in the world. What do you know about your birth experience? Where and how you were born?

K: I've no idea . . . hospital I think. It was normal as far as I know. Mum told me once that it took ages and she was drugged to the eyeballs by the time I was born. She's never understood anyone wanting to take drugs.

C: How old was your brother when you were born?

K: Ten.

C: Do you know anything else about your birth?

K: Nothing.

C: What do you know about your early years?

K: Mum never talks about things like that, doesn't look back. I don't remember anything before I started school but that felt like when my life began. I loved everything about school. The smell of big crayons; that first blank page in an exercise book waiting to be filled; the smell of a new bag, wooden ruler, and a new pencil case with everything unused; a new school year with classrooms smelling of fresh paint and unspoilt colourful posters on the walls; story books I took home to read, lying on my bed with my legs up against the wall; lunch boxes and plastic flasks with cartoon characters on; using my first computer and finding games you could play with all kinds of weird and funny sounds; dinner ladies who would give you "seconds" and games in the playground.

Karen looks out of the window as she's speaking and her whole face is alight with a smile, she's still again.

C: You look happy as you talk about school and I can imagine your joy as that young girl. What about home during those young years?

Karen's fingers immediately sneak under her blouse and I can see her scratching her forearm.

K: Home was a nightmare that I escaped from by going to school. I've thought about it over the past few weeks and I realise that I need to talk about my father, I think that's part of why it was difficult for me to come to this appointment.

C: What would make that easier?

K: I think what you said last time about "opening the can of worms a bit at a time" helps . . . anyway he was a binge drinker and he'd come home from the pub and throw his weight around. He'd control himself if mum was around. My earliest memory was of him ranting and raving and hitting out at Roy, if she wasn't around. One time was terrifying when Roy decided he'd had enough and he hit him back. They were like two bull elephants fighting to the death. Roy gave him a bloody nose and a black eye. I must've been about seven. My brother was babysitting and he'd let me stay up to watch a band on television that we both wanted to see. I'd been feeling very grown up. My dad came in drunk and picked a fight with him. A chair got broke, mugs went flying off the table, and I sat with hands over my ears terrified by the smell and sight of blood splattered on the carpet. Mum was out at bingo. I remember she came home and shouted when she saw the state of them and the house. I'd already gone to sit out of the way at the top of the stairs and made a quick exit to bed. I never saw them get into a fight again.

C: That must have been very frightening.

K: It got worse for me . . . dad would slap me around a bit if I did something wrong . . . I got used to that and made myself scarce . . . got good at keeping out of the way . . . I don't know if I want to talk about anything else about him today.

C: What is happening inside of you when you say that?

K: I feel small, as if I have no words . . . I feel a bit like an iceberg with a small part of me showing and something enormous that was frozen, hidden underneath. I'm afraid that if that ever thaws out, I won't be able to control it.

C: It sounds as if you coped with the past by hiding some very painful feelings. Have you ever talked to anyone about what happened to you?

K: I had to talk to my sister-in-law, Becks, after my nephew and niece were born. I had to protect them from my dad. I knew he could hurt them. I'd tried to warn Roy but he's such a dickhead and wouldn't believe me. He's a piss pot like Dad but I don't think he'd ever hurt his kids. Becks and I go back a long way and she knew I was telling the truth. She sorted it out. I told mum about stuff when I was sixteen, about why I wanted to leave home. She didn't believe me either and tried to talk me out of leaving. When she realised I would go anyway, she supported me getting out of the house and gave me a letter for social services so I could get funding for a place on my own. I don't know why she stayed with him, except if anything, he was a bit in awe of her. He treated her okay most of the time. Thing is, my dad was well known locally for helping people out, if the council wouldn't come and fix something. He was a good builder, worked as a foreman for a large construction company, and he'd do small building jobs for people on the estate, at the pub, and the social club. He was a local councillor for a time. Everyone talked about him as "good ole Joe". He was like two different people. I used to silently hate him. Maybe, it's that old rage that's frozen inside still.

The whole time Karen speaks the foot of her crossed leg is moving up and down and she's scratching her forearms, picking at the skin on her forehead, pulling on her ear lobe, constantly restless.

C: I have a suggestion of an exercise which can sometimes help to release anger towards someone who's hurt you. It involves imagining that person on the stage of an empty theatre, of which you are in charge. You are the director/producer of your own theatre. You can imagine anything happening to that person and the audience can be filled with anyone you want or no-one. It's a way of working with negative feelings without anyone being hurt. It takes a few minutes and then you need to do the whole exercise again, but the second time imagine something good happening to the same person. It can be a way of reclaiming your power back, if you've felt bullied by someone. What do you think? Would you be willing to have a go?

K: I don't think I'd be able to think of something good happening to him but I'm willing to do the first bit and see how I feel. I know I've carried this around far too long.

C: Okay. I'd like you to put both of your feet on the floor to ground yourself here. Then, close your eyes and imagine that you're sitting somewhere in a theatre so that you can see everything happening on stage. You might want to have other people in the audience with you, to support you, to witness what goes on, to be part of the whole experience. Imagine who you would put there and where they would sit. Then you can set the scene on the stage, think about what you want to happen and how you'll introduce the actors, the people you want to be there. You're completely in control, in charge; everything that happens is directed by you. Give yourself a few minutes to experience the whole performance and when you are ready, come back into the room. You can share what happens with me or not as you choose. Then we can talk about the second part after that. You have the stage.

Karen is surprisingly still and absorbed in what is going on. Her eyes are moving underneath her closed lids. She looks pale except where she's been scratching at her forehead which is red and blotchy. She always looks smart and today wears a grey pinstripe skirt and jacket with a royal blue long sleeved blouse. She always looks good and her hair is well cut to frame her face. She's a fast moving, fast talking, feisty, young woman. After several minutes Karen opens her eyes.

C: As you come back into this room, notice a colour and shape that will help you to return and feel grounded here.

Karen takes a while to look around the room, look at me, and really come back to the present moment.

K: I didn't know if I could or even would really want to do that, just to be in a place with my father was so horrible. I began by filling the theatre with lots of local people who admired him, people who would say to me, how wonderful he was and how much he'd helped them. I wanted them all to see who he really was. I'd been seen as the rebellious "difficult" daughter. Then as it was time to begin, I felt really sick, not scared, but angry. I didn't want to be anywhere near him. I wanted to vomit hatred all over him. I wanted him to taste the bitterness that I'd felt in my own throat and mouth. I wanted to watch everyone's reaction when they heard what he did. What he was capable of doing. He wasn't the kind, helpful, mate from round the corner. So the stage became a court of law and he was put in the dock. There was a judge running the court and a police-woman came on stage and gave evidence in great detail and told every-one exactly what he did to Roy and to me; everything. I didn't have to give evidence. The judge held up three placards, each with a different punishment written on it. Everyone had three lights to choose from and they had to press one of them to decide the outcome. I wanted justice. I wanted him to see the people who admired him decide what to do with him. The three punishments were: to be put in prison for twenty-five years (blue light); to be thrashed to death with a nine tails (red light); or to have his penis cut off and for him to have to eat it (green light). They nearly all voted for the third one, the theatre was lit up with a green glow. I did too. My brother and my mother had been watching from the side of the stage as neither of them believed what he was capable of. Then my brother had to tie up his hands. An executioner type of man came in and cut off his penis, cut it up into pieces, and made him eat it. He gagged on every mouthful as it was forced down. He couldn't do anyone any harm anymore.

C: How do you feel now?

K: Weirdly, I do feel a sense of relief that they all know what he was capa-ble of, what he did. That he can't hurt anyone anymore. I feel safe for the first time. I don't think I've ever believed he isn't going to hurt me again. He looked so pathetic at the end.

C: It was very brave of you to do this.

K: It was very hard and my head is throbbing. Do you mind if I take a paracetamol?

C: Would you like a glass of water with it?

K: Yes please.

I get Karen a glass of water as she takes a couple of paracetamol, from her bag.

C: Do you feel able to continue?

K: Yes, I think so. Do you think I'm awful . . . what I imagined?

C: Honestly, I don't. There's a strong boundary between what we imag-ine and what we do. One of the reasons that fairy tales are so important to children and adults alike is that they normalise our worst and best feel-ings, thoughts, images, and behaviour. Sometimes those boundaries get badly blurred for people and for many reasons they do act out those unthinkable behaviours, usually because it's happened to them, and maybe that's what your father did. What you were doing was safe because it stayed in your imagination. It sounds to me that the only person you have hurt is yourself. I want to support you not doing that and if this is part of a process that will help you to make different choices in your life then that's great.

K: I see what you mean. I've thought I was bad to have hateful feelings and thoughts. I've never thought about how important fairy tales are. Is that why they're so macabre?

C: I think so. Children love them and even enjoy being scared and such stories have been told around camp fires for hundreds of years. It's only in recent times that we've sanitised them but I think they normalise a wide spectrum of human feelings, thoughts, and rich imagination.

K: I quite like horror films, maybe that's why.

C: Do you think you could do the same again only now imagine some-thing good happening on the stage?

K: I didn't think I could but now I may be able to, for myself, not for him.

C: Good for you. Well, when you're ready, perhaps you can choose the same or a different theatre and again, if you want to have other people there as a support, you can. This time, I want you to imagine something good happening to the people that were involved in the last performance.

K: Okay.

Karen shut her eyes and she is again very still and takes her time. Her deep frown from before is gone. Eventually, she opens her eyes.

C: Again Karen, I invite you to notice a colour or shape in this room to ground you back here in the present moment.

K: The theatre seats were empty. I imagined that the four of us were sitting at a table in a very nice restaurant, something I can never remember us doing.

Karen looks sad and then suddenly sobs and takes a tissue. She cries loudly and there is a loud howl that comes from deep within her that was heart-felt. She continues to cry for several minutes, blows her nose, and wipes her eyes, face, and chin. There were wet patches on her shirt where tears had fallen.

K: I'm sorry. You must think I'm such a wimp. I don't allow myself to cry normally.

C: I don't, Karen. I think you are very brave to have opened the can of worms a bit today. Do you need anything or do you have any questions about what we've done today?

K: Do you honestly think that what he did to me was something that happened to him?

C: I think people learn that kind of behaviour from somewhere and quite often from their experiences in childhood. That's how abuse can carry on, until someone, like you, says, "no more".

K: I've never thought of that. To be honest I don't think of him at all if I can help it. It was so weird to think of doing something "nice" as a family that included him. It was rare for us to do anything together once Roy left.

C: In my experience, however badly someone may choose to behave, they are rarely all bad.

K: That's too much for me to believe just yet.

C: You've worked hard today and it's nearly time to end. I like to give people something to do at home in between sessions. I hope what I suggest might be enjoyable. I'm aware that the main aim of your coming for counselling is to stop using cocaine. It sometimes helps us to stop doing something if we are rewarding ourselves at the same time. I think it's great that you've been to a couple of sessions of auricular acupuncture and hope that you might continue with that. My suggestion is that you think about anything else you could do for yourself that would be nurturing. It could be things like: buying one single beautiful flower; a scented candlelight bath, if you have a bath; a reflexology treatment; buying some special perfume; going out to the cinema with a friend; whatever you really enjoy that would take you out of work mode. In the same way, it might be helpful to become more aware of the triggers for you using cocaine and think if there is anything nurturing you can do instead. You deserve the best possible support to help you in this process. I have here somewhere a list of mood boosting foods, which might help with the withdrawal symptoms you're getting from cutting down.

I get a sheet out of my drawer and give it to Karen.

K: I like the sound of that as homework and this looks useful. Anything that helps with the swings of mood from gloom to hyper would be good.

We make an appointment in two weeks because Karen is away working in New York for a week. I walk down to the office with her and she seems a bit calmer.

Second session of counselling

Karen had an appointment two weeks after her last session because of a working trip to New York but then she cancelled two more appointments so it's five weeks since we met last. I collect her from the waiting room and again she's very apologetic about the cancellations. She's wearing a very chic dark red skirt suit with a black blouse underneath. It's warm so she takes off her jacket and hangs it up on the peg near the door. She quickly takes her seat and sits perched on the edge of her seat.

K: I'll understand if you can't continue to work with me when I keep cancelling. It's just very hard to get away from work in the present economic chaos.

C: I understand a little about the world you're working in and its unpredictability. What concerns me Karen is you being able to give this time to yourself for your recovery and maybe we need to focus on that today. What do you think?

K: I left last time feeling resolved, even a little calmer. The trip to New York was very stressful. I increased the cocaine again during that time, which made it harder to come back to the counselling. If I'm really honest with you that may have been part of the reason I cancelled the last two sessions. It's getting harder to keep to a lower maintenance level. I slept long and hard this weekend and I've got it back down to a couple of grams a day but I feel like shit and I'm having to drag myself to work, which is not like me.

C: I want to support you in this difficult process, but I can't help you if you're not here. I know you gave me some notice each time you cancelled but you're taking up a regular slot. I need a firm commitment from you in order to offer you another appointment.

K: I understand. You've already been very patient.

C: The hardest part of this process for you *is* to make this commitment and I'm not sure where you are with that. What do you think?

K: I don't want to let you down again.

C: That's great *but* the most important person you need *not* to let down is yourself.

I see tears fill Karen's eyes

K: I'm so scared that I can't do this. I'm used to doing anything I set myself but this fucking drug seems to have me all over the place, tying me in knots in every nerve of my body. I want to scream when night after night I can't sleep. I walk round and round. I run. I go to the gym. I try sooooo hard to run away from it but that craving . . . I want it so much and it blots out *everything* else. The worst part is I get to thinking that it's all okay . . . I can easily do it tomorrow or the next day. I can beat this any time I want . . . and the worst part, particularly since coming here . . . I *know* that's a lie.

Karen makes the heaviest sigh.

K: More than anything else, I need to stop this agonising craving. I can't remember not being preoccupied with the next fix, where the needles are, and how many and how much I have left. What if either of my dealers gets arrested? What if I get too ill to get supplies in? What if I lose my job and can't afford to buy it anymore? Hundreds of questions fill my mind when I should be sleeping. I have to beat this but I'm soooo tired.

C: This is all the pain that you are working hard to stop but it's going to take time. It will get better and it will stop but that isn't going to happen this week, next week . . . What's important is that you don't have to do this on your own. Will you commit to coming back here even if you've increased your intake again?

K: . . . Okay. Do you really not mind seeing me if I'm doing that?

C: I know some counsellors don't like working with clients who are using. We're at the beginning of this process and I don't expect anything from you at this time except that you turn up weekly. We've got three more sessions after this and I want to see you weekly for those three weeks so that we can finish the work together that we've started and for now that seems to be about you committing to this process and accepting help to do that. What do you think?

K: I promise I'll do my absolute best to come.

C: Well, that's good enough for me Karen. What we talked about as your homework . . . did you have a chance to think about and do anything to nurture yourself?

K: I've been for another acupuncture session and I like the woman doing it. I think it's beginning to have an effect. Also, this weekend, I booked a reflexology session. Becks had some with a friend who's training in it at college and she gave me her number. She was very keen on it. Also, I took that list of happy foods, as I call it, to New York, I began to think about what I eat and made an effort to have healthy breakfasts, even if I'm in a meeting. I've been taking more cereal bars for snacks. The fact that I'm even thinking about what might be "good for me" is big.

C: I agree. It's all about consciously creating good health, so well done. How do you take care of yourself normally as regards food and drinking?

K: I drink socially but it's not a problem, if I drink more than one glass of anything alcoholic, I feel queasy. I drink fruit juices rather than wine or lager. I drink lots of coffee at work, probably too much. I've always eaten easy to prepare foods but generally lots of salads, omelettes, pizza slices, and grilled fish. From sixteen, I worked in a supermarket to earn money to get myself through college and then university so I had access to a wide variety of easy to prepare foods. These days, I actually like cooking up pasta and adding nuts and things. I put meals together very fast and usually eat in front of the computer or while I'm watching the money channels, which isn't ideal. I do eat chocolate and other sweet things on the run. I seem to exist on nervous energy which means that I hardly ever put on weight but I eat enough not to be underweight as I was in teenage years.

C: What sounds good is that you're observing yourself and your behaviour and that is one of the steps out of addiction.

K: Do you think so?

C: I do.

K: That gives me a flutter in my stomach that maybe it's possible.

C: Would you be willing to talk a bit about how you got into drugs?

K: When Roy left home, I was about eight. My dad was a nightmare. When mum wasn't around, he'd take his anger out on me and slap me around for the slightest thing. I kept out of his way and spent a lot of time in my room but that seemed to annoy him too. As soon as I could, I'd hang with an older crowd that played out on the estate. We'd go back to anyone's flat, when their parents were out. There was an older friend and when Becks and me was about eleven, we used to go to her flat, play music, and drink cider. Sometimes we'd smoke dope. I never really liked smoking nicotine. We'd smoke a bong and it felt cool, the whole ritual thing. A year or so on, we'd sneak into clubs late on, so we didn't pay anything, and we'd take E; occasionally LSD. As soon as I reached sixteen, I left home and got a grotty little bedsit in a big house not far away from the school. I stayed on at school and got the job in a supermarket. I couldn't afford to do drugs much, just dope. I was working any shift they'd give me after school and weekends so I could afford to live and make my room as good as I could. It was a space where I felt safe. I was studying hard and knew I wanted to get into university. I got in with different people in the sixth form. I stopped seeing the crowd from the estate except for Becks. I worked hard, got into Imperial College but stayed living in my bedsit, carried on working in the supermarket. Becks started going out with Roy so we stopped seeing so much of each other for a while. He and I got on okay then. I got to know different people at Uni., got into a druggy crowd rather than the drinkers. It was in my final year when I needed to stay awake to revise, I knew some people who took speed. We'd make up speed bombs and swallow them to get a bigger effect. I couldn't afford to do much then either but I knew I liked the feeling of escaping from reality. Life had an edge just hanging on to enough reality to do okay at work and Uni. but to have somewhere to escape to. I got used to keeping everything together that way. Sometimes, I'd have to take a day off and just sleep to catch up. It was a weird time.

C: Did you see any of your family?

K: I met up with mum in her lunch hour from work most weeks. She was manager of a dress shop not far away from my bedsit. Occasionally, she'd come and have a meal with me after work if I wasn't working. I didn't see my dad. I swore I'd never go back home and I didn't until dad died just over five years ago. Becks got married to Roy and they got their own place, had the kids and I saw them regularly. Roy started drinking too much so I started to visit them when he was at work or at the pub. I saw less and less of him. He seemed to resent me going to university. She and I saw more of each other after she and Roy divorced.

C: What happened after university?

K: After Uni. I got a good job with a bank. They got rid of some of their expensive employees and took on graduates. I did well, took to that life like a duck to water. My one purpose was to get my own flat, my own home. I worked like stink to make enough money to get a deposit together. I took E's at parties occasionally and speed sometimes to keep awake and just got used to not sleeping very much. At the weekends, I'd just sleep for a whole day or even the entire weekend. There were some very dodgy deals at work and a lot of pressure to do things that I completely disagreed with, so as soon as I could I changed job to work with a slightly more kosher bank. I saved every penny I could. I've always been very single minded. Then, I was head hunted for the job I have now, more money, more responsibility, and even less sleep. As I said before, at twenty-nine, I was able to buy my own one-bedroom flat in Docklands. I thought I'd feel secure but it didn't work like that. I became more anxious, scared of losing everything. It didn't take me long to spend some of that hard earned cash on cocaine. My life filled up with work and I was constantly tuned in and attached to phones and computer screens; meetings from 6.00 a.m. until 8.00 p.m.; drinks afterwards. I loved the adrenaline rush of the chase after bigger and bigger deals. Problem is, people then expect even more from you and there's always someone waiting to sit in your chair. I started to take more and more cocaine; began to inject it to protect my nose; didn't want people to find out even though there's a real culture of drugs in the banking business.

C: It sounds exhausting. Do you enjoy it?

K: I love it when I win. I like the challenge, the repartee, and the humour. You don't get to know anyone properly, we're competing with each other, but it's fun. I'm good at it, I think fast and am used to taking responsibility, so decisions come easy. I think I have a flare for following where the money is or where it's going to be. I keep my ears and eyes open. Recently, I've been surprised that I enjoy mentoring the young people coming in. I get a kick when they win too. My newish boss is a bit of an arsehole 'cos he takes all the credit with "upstairs" and drops me in it if it goes wrong. There's another manager who I first worked with and he's an ally, occasionally he and I chat, and he can't stand "ole buggerlugs". I trust him and believe me that's a rarity. He would fight my corner if needed. I'm not bad at office politics and strategy; it's another way of surviving and winning.

C: You're very animated when you talk about your work.

K: It's very important to me. I know it's not something I could do for many more years without being burnt out but I'm still learning every day and I like that challenge. I need to find a way to do it without thinking I can only do it with cocaine. I know that's not true now. I do realise it can work against me and cause me to take too many risks, with other people's money. That's not right. I'm in danger of losing my judgement which will lose me my job. I've made small mistakes in the last year or two. I've found them in time and had to do a shitload of wheeling and dealing to get back on track. One mistake, about eight months ago, nearly cost me my job. I took a week off and pretended that I was ill. I've never done that before but I got scared, really scared and this one a few months ago that brought me here, that was the closest I've come to a real disaster.

C: I've got a clear picture from what you've told me now. We talked about a referral to a non-residential Rehab. Centre after these sessions. I can recommend one drugs counsellor who I know runs an evening support group. What do you think?

K: Is it a man or a woman?

C: The counsellor is a woman called Mary Chase and I've occasionally referred people on to her. I've heard good feedback about her work in this area. Also, if you don't want to work with her, she's very well fixed to suggest other specialist drug therapists in London. I think it's important that you connect with the therapist first in some individual sessions but that you work with someone who could offer you an opportunity to move into a weekly support group which some people find helpful. What do you think?

K: It took all my effort to come here and even this I've messed up because of work. I'm not good at accepting help.

C: I know you're used to standing on your own feet, you've been very independent, but it's really tough to come off cocaine. I believe strongly that you need good support from other people who know exactly what it's like and also know all the tricks of deception that can take you right back to it again.

K: You're not wrong about that. I know I'm my own worst enemy. I've thought about it and I'm willing to have a go. I'd like to finish these sessions with you first. I know the time has come to get myself straight. I'm losing my cool at work, snapping at everyone. I've been feeling down and sleep; well, during the week, sleep is something that is completely fucked up for me despite the sleeping pills.

C: Have they helped at all?

K: Sometimes, if I go to the gym and wear myself out.

C: I notice that you scratch at the skin on your forehead and forearms.

K: I know I pick at my skin. I get restless, agitated and fidgety, always have. I don't even realise I'm doing it. It's a continuation from when I used to cut myself. It does relieve the tension. I've read that it releases a drug in the body which dulls the pain, emotional and physical.

C: I just want to reiterate again Karen that you've achieved much in your life despite what sounds like an abusive and very difficult family life. I wonder if you're able to really appreciate how well you've done. You learnt as a child, to survive and protect yourself as best you could. You removed yourself from an abusive situation at home. You worked hard to provide a safe place for yourself as a teenager. At the same time, you achieved a high level of academic success. You have a very successful career that you enjoy and you've provided a secure home for yourself. You've kept in touch with family members who are important to you. You look fantastic and dress really well and obviously take good care of yourself in that respect. I believe you have all the resources you need to come off cocaine and the fact that you're here means that a large part of you wants to make this change. Can you celebrate what you've achieved?

K: When you put it like that, I suppose I've achieved a lot.

C: It's important for you to remember that through this process. You can be one of the best supports for yourself. Maybe you could create a poster for yourself that you display in a prominent place to remind you of your successes?

K: I could do. There's still this inner chaos that I deal with in a crazy way.

C: I think part of what will help you deal with that successfully is first to celebrate your successes and then to realise that it's okay to have limitations, whether we decide to work on them or not. We all make mistakes, it's how we learn. We need to.

K: I suppose we do. Maybe one day I'll stop punishing myself for being a real "fuck up".

C: I don't really know where we get this idea that we have to be perfect. Welcome to the rest of the human race.

K: Mmmm.

Karen smiles and again, I notice her foot stops moving.

C: For many reasons, some of which were to do with your "survival", you've chosen to use cocaine and choices are something we can change but first we need to become aware of what we're doing. You say that when you scratch at your skin, you're not aware of doing it. It's a first step in being able to change something for us to begin to become an active observer of our own behaviour rather than reacting automatically. I want to suggest that during the coming week you begin to develop that awareness by really noticing the choices you make about even small things. If someone offers you a drink, ask yourself if you want a hot drink, for example, tea, coffee, herbal tea; a cold drink, for example, a juice, water, fizzy drink, alcoholic drink. Stop for a moment and think about the fact that you have choices which could include something you've never tried. When you travel to work or home, think about if you want to walk, bus, tube, or take a taxi. You can choose to do it the same or differently. If you shop for something, could you choose to shop somewhere new? When you go to the gym, could you do your exercises on different machines and/or in a different order? It's about making our choices more conscious and maybe being willing to risk making a change. What do you think?

K: I'm a terrible creature of habit, especially at the gym. I get quite miffed if someone is on *my* rowing machine. I end up doing most things in exactly the same way.

C: That can be very comforting but when you are working towards making a big and healthier change in your life, it can help to build a toleration to risking making smaller changes and noticing how that feels. It's also important for you to support yourself by nurturing yourself in healthy ways and noticing how that feels. So, these two things: first, noticing that you have choices and can risk different choices; and second, being willing to actively nurture yourself in positive ways. These are important tools to help you build the confidence to know you can do this. I want you to consider an idea that some people have found useful. You talked of an inner chaos and I'd like you to imagine building a solid brick pier in your very centre, rooted like a tree trunk down into the ground. I'll draw it.

On a pad, I draw a picture that is like a tall chimney made of bricks, a greater diameter at the bottom and small at the top. I draw a stick person through which this runs and draw roots growing down from the brick pier into the ground below.

C: An inner strength grows from you being centred in yourself rather than in cocaine. You need to be grounded back into your own body and senses. This was the place you needed to escape from as a child and now you need to get it back. These individual bricks that make up this solid centre are what will help you. I want you to imagine that whenever you do something that you enjoy, particularly for your body: listen to relaxing music; dance; sing; prepare a nice meal which you fully experience by eating it in pleasant surroundings rather than in front of the computer; massage your hands and feet with some luxurious smelling cream; read the poster celebrating your many successes; even when you give yourself these counselling sessions; you are putting *in* a brick to make this brick pier more substantial. Every time you do something negative for yourself: take more drugs than you've agreed with yourself; spend too long at one go in front of the computer; drink too much coffee; scratch your face, or arms, or anything else that you know makes you more tense or agitated, it's as if you are taking *out* a brick from your centre, which then makes your inner self less stable and strong. Do you see what I mean?

K: I get it, it's logical and that appeals to me. Can I take that picture with me?

C: Of course you can. This is a two pronged attack on those old habits. You empower yourself by being more able to risk changing and you strengthen your resolve and self-esteem by nurturing yourself. What do you think?

K: I can see it. I've worked on making the outside of me okay but that inner core has had a lot of bricks missing for a long time. I can also see that I needed to leave myself and my home to be safe. I didn't have a choice then did I?

C: You made the best choice for yourself at the time, to survive.

K: It's been my security to buy my own home, to have a safe place, to have a good income, nice clothes, stuff . . . but that's on the outside . . . I really get this . . . I need to come home to my body, my senses, my feelings . . . everything I've worked hard to block out. The drugs have kept me from myself . . . I really get this . . . I've done it on the outside but not on the inside . . . but can I do it?

C: You were half way there when you came through this door for the first time, because you want to change this. Now it's about finding the will and the support to do it.

K: Okay, this picture will help to remind me.

C: It seems as if you know what the cocaine has been for you?

K: Yes, I can see it's been a perfect distraction, a way of not looking into that centre at all. I've used it to dissociate from my inner world, the feelings, the past, the pain, and, most of all, my body.

C: But it was a way of surviving?

K: Back to that "can of worms". Next time, I think I might want to talk more about that with you. I'll see how I feel.

C: Could you bring along some photos of you as a child, some that might be important memories for you?

K: I've never looked at old family photos. I know mum has some. I could ask her. I don't very often go to the house. I'll think about it.

C: As children we find the best way to get through, trauma, loss, unhappiness. Then, as adults, if we're fortunate enough we reach a point when we're strong enough or aware enough to realise that those coping strategies don't work for us anymore and we need to change. Does this help you understand why drugs might have been very appealing to you as you grew up?

K: You almost make it sound as if it was a good thing.

C: Well, it wasn't good that you felt that your survival depended on dissociation from yourself but given the circumstances that you were in, survival becomes everything until you're in a position to take care of yourself in a different way.

K: I can see that I've been running away from reality and relationships and I've been filling up the emptiness of that with work and a relentless drive towards perfection. Everything on the outside has to be perfect: work, my flat, even my clothes. I spend a lot of time on keeping everything in perfect order. That both fills my head and helps with the restless agitation in my body from the cocaine and the cravings when I'm not taking it. Just thinking about it makes me feel exhausted. I don't want to stay on this treadmill. I can see that if I do, it will keep moving faster and faster and there's a danger I'll be thrown off.

Karen looks suddenly pale and thoughtful as she looks out of the window and we sit for a few moments in silence.

K: Do you believe I can change this?

C: If you're willing to commit to yourself and get support. I'm sure you can.

K: The alternative doesn't look so good does it?

C: Life has a lot more to offer than being on a treadmill.

Karen's eyes well up with tears and she takes a tissue immediately from the tissue box on the table beside her. She immediately stops the tears and blows her nose.

K: I feel as if my body has always been "on guard", waiting for an attack, waiting to see what mood the people are in around me.

C: It must have been very hard for you not to have a place where you felt safe, especially as a small child in your own home.

K: I hope that I'm ready for this now.

C: It sounds as if you came here partly because you wanted to keep your job but you need to decide to do it now for yourself. It will take time and commitment but I believe you're worth it. What do you believe?

K: I believe that if I don't do this for myself, my dad's still in control and I can't stand the thought of that.

C: Do you know anything about his parenting?

K: His dad was a mean old sod. I remember him. He drank and used to knock my gran around. My dad never laid a finger on my mum. He took it out on us instead.

C: These things are learnt in families and can be passed down like eye and hair colour, until someone like you has the courage and will to decide to stop it and say *no* to treating other people or themselves abusively.

K: I haven't thought about it like that. Perhaps that's what stops me from getting into a long term relationship. My brother's a drinker and began to push Becks around until she decided to throw him out, she wasn't about to stand for that. Thankfully he has much less influence on my nephew and niece than she does. Becks is a good mum and they're doing okay.

C: They've got your support too.

K: Becks and me, we've always been there for each other.

C: It's almost time to finish. Do you have any questions or comments about today?

K: No, I honestly didn't believe this counselling would be any good. I've always known it's down to me but I feel as if I've learnt a lot today. I get that I have to find the will to make this change.

C: I think it's important for you to come to the counselling next week and the following two sessions so that we both know that you can commit to this. I believe that's what having the will, is all about. No cancellations. No more excuses. This is your time and *you matter*. This change matters. Our working together, matters. I don't want you to lose any sessions because of another cancellation. What do you think?

K: I think that this has suddenly become very important to me.

C: Does that mean you're important to you?

Karen smiles.

K: I think I've always been a survivor but I can see that isn't the same as *living*. My ability to be . . . myself . . . whatever that is . . . has frankly been terrifyingly missing . . . and the cost is too bloody expensive.

C: I look forward to seeing you next week then.

We both smile and make an appointment for the following week. I watch her walk away, smart, confident, and beautiful and I feel moved by the courage and beauty on the inside that she may yet discover. She's entered into this process with such trust considering what she's experienced.

Third session of counselling

Karen did cancel our third session but rang up to see if there was a cancellation the same week on the Friday and I was able fit her in. I greet her in the waiting room and as we walk down the hallway, she is apologising profusely for yet another cancellation. She takes off her jacket and carefully hangs it on the back of her chair.

K: I'm so glad you could fit me in. I cancelled because something came up at work . . . I could've asked someone else to handle it . . . I began to realised how scared I was about talking about stuff. After some wrestling with myself, I phoned yesterday to see if you had a cancellation. I even asked a colleague to cover for me. To prepare for today, I went back to the house last night and selected some old photos. Then, this morning I forgot to bring them but I'll bring them next time. At the house, I spent a few moments in my old room and allowed myself to remember. It was the hardest thing not to up the cocaine when I got home. I went to the gym and did the longest work out I've ever done. I was so knackered that I even slept. Normally, even with the sleeping tablets, I don't go off to sleep for hours.

C: You did well. I'm really glad to see you this week, not quite as we planned, but you got here, that's the main thing and we can take a look at the photos next time.

K: Thanks.

C: I have a suggestion about a way you could work on what happened with your dad. It's something other people have found helpful when considering past trauma. What I propose is that you think of an experience that you had that was particularly painful and you talk about it as if you are an observer, looking in through a window or door to wherever it happened. Then you're allowed to go into the room and change things. That might mean sending your father or anyone else out of the room. It might mean that you sit with the young Karen, whatever suits you both. You could imagine comforting her; talking to her; whatever you feel that she needs from you to feel supported and safe. You might want to explain why these things happen; tell her that it isn't her fault; anything that you can do to reassure, support, and nurture her. Finally, I want you to reassure her that you, as you are now, are willing to take care of her and make sure this doesn't happen again. Don't plan too much now. The main thing is that you get the idea of what's involved. What do you think?

K: I think that would make it easier.

C: It's another way of dealing with the past, a little at a time, in a way that involves the person you've become.

K: I can see that. It still feels scary and I'm most afraid that I can't help her. What if I don't know what to say or do? I felt powerless then but there's a part of me that feels powerless now.

C: Think of how you've comforted your nephew or niece at some point and tell me about that.

K: Emmm . . . I took Graham out to the shops once and we saw a cyclist knocked off his bike and he was screaming. A couple of people rushed to help. Despite being shocked myself, I took Graham away into a nearby park and explained that the ambulance was on its way and they would take the cyclist to hospital and make him better. He was very upset . . . Another time, I was at Beck's when my brother brought Emily and Graham home and he started going off on one about child support, as usual. Becks had left me in the garden, sun bathing, when she went to open the door and she told the kids to come out into the garden without saying I was there. Normally, I'd have joined in with the argument and it would have got a lot worse but as he didn't know I was there, I played some games with the kids outside until he'd left which took their minds off it all completely.

C: So it sounds as if you have all the right skills.

K: Okay, I'll have a go. Can I just go to the loo first?

C: Of course. You know where it is?

K: Yeah.

Karen's hands are very shaky as she gets up and goes off to the loo. She takes her bag and I can see when she comes back that she's brushed her hair and renewed her lipstick.

C: Ready?

K: As much as I'll ever be.

C: Sit comfortably, close your eyes and imagine an occasion when "little Karen" would most have needed adult support. I want you to imagine that you are a safe distance away, looking on, with the knowledge that you can go in and help at any time. "Where is she?" and "What is she wearing?"

Karen closes her eyes. She lightly bites down on her bottom lip and takes a few moments before speaking.

K: She's in her bedroom, fast asleep, wearing a pink nightie with blue teddy bears on.

C: Imagine being you now, looking in, and describe what happens?

K: The "Freak" comes in to her room with his drunken tooth smile, in his pyjamas. Her brother's left home and her mother's staying over with Gran who's ill. She's half asleep and he sits on the bed and strokes her hair. He's hardly ever soft like that with her even when he's sober. Many times when he touches her, it's to shake her, grab her arm too tightly, push her out of the way, or hold her hand too tightly and crunch her fingers together painfully as he pulls her along the road with him. She's enjoying the gentle touch and his soft, wheedling voice. This is the dad of her dreams. He tells her he loves her. She drifts into and out of sleep. He tells her she's too hot and she should take off her nightie. He helps her out of it and she relaxes, naked, in a sleepy haze, even though she can smell whiskey on his breath. She's used to that and sometimes, it makes him "nice". He continues to stroke her hair, arms, legs, all the time telling her how beautiful she is and how much he loves her. That never happened and she enjoys it and again drifts into and out of sleep and feels safe. He tells her that he has a new game to play with her and "Daddy's little friend". He tells her a little story about "his friend", that if she strokes it very gently it'll grow. He shows her and she knows somewhere deep inside that this is "wrong" but she's confused by his wheedling voice, which is new, different, soft, but beginning to be threatening. She's fully awake now and tells him she doesn't want to play. His smile tightens and he tells her she has to play. She's scared now and remembers that there's no-one else around. He tells her that if she doesn't play this game, he'll hurt mummy badly. She does what he says and counts the blue teddy bears. She gets to thirty . . . I have to go in to her now.

C: So do what you need to do.

K: I'm going into the room and I'm pulling him off the bed on to the floor and covering his penis. I'm shouting at him. "You're a fucking freak, get up, pull up your fucking trousers, get out, and leave her alone. Fuck off and never come back, never, you hear." I pick up a half size cricket bat from the floor and see him out of the door with a loud crack on his back and put a chair up against it so he can't get back in. Little Karen is shaking and sobbing. I sit next to her and say over and over again: "He's totally wrong to do that to you . . . he won't do it again. It's not a game, it's wrong for him to do that to you. He's doing it because whiskey makes him do bad things sometimes. I'm here and I'm going to protect you from this ever happening again. You're safe now. You haven't done anything wrong, he has, this is something inside him, it's got nothing to do with you. He'll never get you on his own again without me being here. I'll protect you." I sit next to her holding her. She's still sobbing but she stops shaking. She asks me who I am and I tell her. I tell her about my life, a bit about work, my flat which is a safe place, my favourite hat which I bought for a wedding which has two peacock feathers in it. I talk to her until I feel her heart has stopped thumping and she's calmer. We sit in silence . . . She tells me about her friend Becks who'd just got a white mouse and a cage with a wheel for her birthday, and her friend David who sits next to her in her class. That afternoon they'd used some big coloured pens and were allowed to write all over a special desk, it felt naughty but they were allowed by their teacher, Mrs Shamsie . . .

Karen stops, stays silent for a few moments and opens her eyes.

C: When you're ready ground yourself back in this room here, today, and notice a shape and colour somewhere in this room.

We sit quietly together for a bit.

K: I feel really knackered . . . shattered. I hate the frigging Freak. I wish I'd had me to do that then, except I'd have killed the fucker.

C: Fortunately, you do have yourself to protect you now.

K: I'm glad he's dead. He died painfully in hospital of sclerosis of the liver and he deserved it. I hated him so much. All the locals saw him as "good old Joe" . . . made me sick.

C: How old was little Karen?

K: I was eight when it started. He never did it when mum was around. I'd wedge a chair against the door handle if I knew mum was out or away but if he was in that mood, he'd force it open and then beat me where it didn't show. Once, when I knew mum was going to stay away, I asked if I could sleep over with Becks. He told me he'd kill mum if I did that again, or if I told her, or anyone else about it. I knew he was capable of doing that. He was like two people, "the Freak" and "good old Joe". She'd get angry with me for being "moody" with him. He raped me when I was ten. I stole a kitchen knife from Woolworths, waited until he came into my room again and stuck it in his leg. He had to drive himself to hospital, don't know what he told them. He called me a monster and the coward stopped then. He'd still hit out at me if I did something wrong but he was a bit lighter on the touch, more respectful. I finally told mum about the abuse, when I asked her for the letter to say I wasn't able to live at home, on my sixteenth birthday. She thought I was making it up and wouldn't hear anything against him but after a big argument, she gave me the letter.

C: That was very courageous of you and horrible that you weren't believed.

K: It all came out eventually when Graham and Emily were little. Roy was back living at home after they split up. I told Becks about it to protect the children being on their own in the house with "the Freak". She believed me, knew I wouldn't do anything to harm the children. Roy thinks that I just made it up for attention but Becks made sure he wouldn't leave the children with my dad. Becks talked to mum and got her agreement on that as well. Eventually mum and I discussed it again. She'd never heard of anyone doing such a thing so I gave her stuff to read, and gradually she began to believe me. She found it hard to accept something like that was going on in our own home. She went through a crisis and by that time he was too ill for her to leave even if she wanted to. She won't talk about it much, it makes her feel bad. She's apologised for not protecting me. She feels bad about Roy drinking, that's why she puts up with him, she feels guilty. She's sometimes dealt with things by being a bit of an "ostrich" not really seeing what she doesn't want to believe. Everyone around us used to say how lucky she was to have such a good man who'd help anyone out. She thought he was too strict with us and she'd get angry with him sometimes but she believed he was trying to be a good father. He was good to her. We've probably talked about it more since all this crap with Jimmy Savile, another friggin freak. She knew dad's dad was violent. She realises now that she never questioned why her sister in law would never have anything to do with any of the family and eventually went off to live in Australia without a word. Dad never talked about her. Mum thinks maybe something like that may have happened to her. Then, his other sister was knocked down and killed by a car. It makes you question everything.

C: I'm so sorry that this happened to you. How have you felt about doing this today?

K: It's been exhausting but a relief to talk about it in this way. It's given me some relief, along with the theatre thing. I suppose you've come across this before.

C: Unfortunately, I have but what is amazing is how people can move on. You went on to become successful at school, in your job, in your ability to provide for yourself, and create your own home as a safe place. Of course there have been serious costs to you but the fact that you are here means that you intend to minimise those as well.

K: I suppose so. It's weird that counting and numbers became part of what I escaped into. I'd distract myself by counting. I had a night light so I'd feel safe . . . makes you sick doesn't it . . . I would count the flowers on the wallpaper, squares on the carpet, tiny bubbles on the curtains. My enjoyment of school became more like obsession. I saw a way out and took it.

C: Did you talk to anyone else about the abuse?

K: I was scared to say anything after I stabbed my dad. He told me if I told anyone about the rape, he'd hurt mum and he'd make sure I went to a detention centre myself for attacking him. I didn't trust any adults. It took a lot of persuasion to get Becks to believe me and she knows I wouldn't bullshit about something like that. I've only spoken to her, Roy, and mum . . . and now here.

C: Do you feel that there's anything left you would like to have said or done?

K: I can't forgive him for what he did, ever, but I want to put it behind me. I know there was a time when I loved him but that was just worn away. I feel nothing but contempt for him and his kind.

C: Perhaps being able to put it behind you is enough. Maybe when you have fully taken back your life and you are living in a way that you want to, it may be possible to forgive your dad, for your own sake, not for his.

K: Maybe . . . I feel a long way from that while I'm allowing myself to be held captive by this bloody cocaine habit.

C: If the cocaine was a person, what kind of person would it be?

K: A helpful one . . . no . . . I don't mean that . . . God, I see what you mean . . . it would bloody well be like him wouldn't it?

C: I don't know. What do you think?

K: Of course. The wheedling, the friendly smile: "Come and be fucked over." "Let's play a game of make believe." It's a liar, like him. It doesn't *really* give me energy or any kind of escape . . . It's like he's won, the old bastard.

C: That's horrible for you.

K: He taught me to dissociate from my body. I thought it kept me safe. He taught me to hate him and myself and I have. I did have some thoughts that maybe it was something I did, something wrong with me.

C: It wasn't a choice though was it?

K: No, it certainly wasn't that.

C: Well, you did a good job today in protecting little Karen. Now maybe you need to transfer that skill to protecting Karen the adult.

K: I can do that. I *can* do that . . . back to the brick pier. I put your picture on my fridge door. I did have a candlelit bath this week and I did resist upping the white stuff last night despite the cravings being as strong as I've ever known them. Maybe I need to call it "the white Freak". I think that might help me.

C: Have you ever tried any form of relaxation or meditation?

K: I'm so geed up all the time. I don't think I'd be able to do it.

C: It might help when the cravings are bad. Would you like to have a go at a few short breathing meditations before we end today?

K: I'm up for anything if it'll help.

C: I won't do a long one with you, but if I run through a few short ones and you can choose one that might work for you.

K: That sounds good.

C: So, the first one is a few minutes and involves just noticing your breathing in and your breathing out. I'll talk you through it. I want you to close your eyes and put both of your feet on the floor so that you feel as grounded as possible. Make that connection with the floor, with your chair. Make yourself as comfortable as possible.

Karen shuts her eyes and shifts position until she looks comfortable.

C: I want you to give all your weight to the chair and the ground, let yourself feel the ground beneath your feet supporting you completely and let yourself feel the chair holding you safely in this place. Take a few deep breaths into your abdomen. If you want to and it feels comfortable, place one hand just above your navel and take a deep breath in and feel it gradually fill your upper chest, lower chest, and drift down so that it gently pushes out your hand. Just a few deep breaths and then let your breathing return to normal. I'd like you to simply notice your breathing in and your breathing out. You could make your breathing out a little bit longer than your breathing in. This helps us to relax. As you notice your breathing, let yourself again feel that the ground is supporting you and the chair is holding you safely so that you can let go and give a little more weight into the chair and the ground supporting you. As you continue to notice your breathing, just let any thoughts come in and drift off again. Don't stop them or feel you have to do anything except notice your breathing in and your breathing out. Feel fully supported and just allow your breathing to find its own pace. A few more breaths and then, in your own time, ground yourself back here by opening your eyes and noticing a colour and shape in this room.

Karen opens her eyes and smiles.

K: Mmm . . . I don't think I've sat that still for ages.

C: You can do that anywhere any time, even if you take a break, sitting on the loo. It's harder to do it at your desk or in front of a computer. Ready for another one?

K: Yes please.

C: Okay, this one involves a bit more visualisation. None of these are more than a few minutes. So, close your eyes and again, feet flat on the floor feeling the ground supporting you and find a comfortable position and feel held by the chair. Let go of your weight feeling supported by the ground and the chair, and take a few deep breaths into that space just above your navel, and then let your breathing return to an easy pace for you. Notice your breathing in and breathing out. Give yourself all the time you need to take the air in and feel it drifting down through your upper, lower lungs and down into that space, at a slow and easy pace. Find an easy rhythm for your breathing. Now I want you to imagine that you are sitting in a safe and beautiful place, somewhere in nature, maybe beside water. It could be the sea, a bubbling river, a waterfall, in nature some-where that is from your imagination, from a film, or a special place you love, a place where you've felt relaxed and safe. You're sitting being supported by the Earth and your back is against a tree, a rock, a wall. Let yourself imagine that this is your safe place, somewhere you can visit any time. Allow yourself to feel safe, supported, and comfortable. Again, notice your breathing in and breathing out. You can spend a bit longer in this beautiful place, imagining the sun or breeze on your face. Notice the sounds, it may be the wind, birds singing, water flowing, and notice any scents of flowers. As you notice your breathing, feel a connection with this beautiful place. You connect with the world through your breathing in and your breathing out. Find a pace that is restful. Again, any thoughts; let them come in and drift away on the breeze. As you notice your breathing, give your weight more and more to the ground and to this beautiful place . . . After the next few breaths and in your own time, slowly come back here and when you open your eyes, notice a colour and a shape to ground you back here in this room.

Karen takes a bit longer to open her eyes and look around and again smiles.

K: That was easier than the first time.

C: Good. Are you up for one more, a few minutes longer?

K: I am. Have you ever had anyone fall asleep.

C: Only once, in a group and he snored which set someone off giggling. Luckily he woke up at the end without prompting.

K: I sometimes think if I slept deeply enough, I'd never wake up.

C: Drugs like cocaine and speed can make you hugely overdrawn of sleep.

K: I get so exhausted sometimes that I have no choice but to take a whole day, usually a Sunday, and just sleep; that does help.

C: I think that short meditations can be like a "power nap". So, again, close your eyes and this time as you take those first few deep breaths imagine yourself in that beautiful safe place again or a different place if you prefer. Feel yourself supported. You can be sitting against a tree, a rock, a wall. Whatever you imagine that makes this place safe, comfortable, and supportive. Then find that easy pace of breathing and notice your breathing in and your breathing out. Let those thoughts come in and drift right away again. Give your weight to the earth below, feel supported, feel held. Notice each breath. Feel each breath in gradually fill the whole of your lungs and feel the breath out slightly longer to help you relax more deeply. You can make a slight space before each in breath and out breath. I want you to notice any sensations, the breeze or sun on your face, sounds of birds or water, and enjoy that connection between yourself and this beautiful place around you. Then I want you to go a bit deeper into your own self, into your body. As you breathe in, I want you to imagine with your in breath, breathing in peace, this might be in the form of a cloud of colour, the word peace, or just that feeling of peace, but as you breathe in, I want you to imagine breathing in a wave of peace and that this radiates around your body and as you breathe out, I want you to imagine breathing out any anxiety or tension, you could think of that as a grey smoke drifting far up and away into the sky. Feel this circle several times of breathing in a wave of peace and breathing out any anxiety or tension and watching it drift up into the sky, rising far above you. All the time feel yourself giving your weight more and more to the ground, being supported and held in this place outside and this peace flowing around you on the inside . . . with your in breath you can take this wave of peace right down to the tips of your toes or the tips of your fingers. Anywhere you might feel any tension or anxiety, breathe the peace into that place and imagine the tension or anxiety flowing out of you with your out breath . . . Now, I want you to imagine that space around you that is your outer boundary and imagine breathing in this wave of peace into this personal space around you. As you breathe in, imagine this peace soothing the personal space around every part of you and again imagine this space becoming whole and safe again . . . in your own time, return here and when you open your eyes, focus on a colour and a space to ground you back in this room.

Karen takes even longer this time to come back into the room.

K: I rarely feel quiet inside but I was able to feel that this time.

C: I think it would be really valuable for you to be able to do a short meditation, any one of these, on a daily basis. You can gear it to what you most need. You could breathe in peace, joy, love, happiness, courage, calm, confidence as a particular colour or just the word. As you get used to doing it, it does get easier. It can become part of your commitment to yourself, to your recovery, to doing good things for yourself. Remember, each time you do this you get a brick for that solid inner brick pier you're building.

K: Mmm . . . it's remembering to do it, making the time to do it, that's what's difficult. I'm sure it would help.

C: As we begin to see how much we really matter, how worth saving we are, then it becomes easier to make the time to do things that support us.

K: It's hard for me to see that I deserve to get better, that I deserve to have good things when I've messed up so much.

C: Well, none of us are perfect Karen, messing up is part of being human. If we understand why we do the things we do, it's not all down to us, but what we choose to do about it is.

K: It's hard to believe I can turn this around.

C: My experience is that the more we take care of ourselves in small ways, we build up enough positive self-esteem to want to do more.

K: Back to the building bricks again.

C: We've got two more sessions Karen and you've worked very hard today. It might be a good idea for you to contact one of the Rehab. Centres and look at what options they can offer you before we have our last session so that you can move smoothly over to longer term support for yourself. What do you think?

K: That makes sense. My number one priority is to get off, "the white Freak" as soon as possible. This has made me determined.

C: Before we end today. I was wondering if it would be useful for us to talk about relationships next time?

K: You're a hard taskmaster you are. Today was hard but that could be even worse.

C: Why not have a think about what you'd like to use the next two sessions for?

K: I know I have a problem with trust, hardly surprising is it?

C: Not at all surprising. See how you feel next time. What's important is for you to continue to commit to yourself by coming to these last two sessions.

K: You're right. I liked the way we worked with this today. I didn't end up feeling powerless all over again.

C: I'm glad. You've been brilliant at taking care of your outer safety, now you need to take care of your inner safety. I believe you've made the transition to doing that today. You didn't get the support you needed when you were young and it's important for you to get the on-going support you need to recover from your cocaine addiction.

K: Yeah.

C: Shall we make an appointment for next week?

K: Okay.

We make an appointment for the following week and I walk down to the office with Karen to give her a copy of the scripts of the short meditations that she can then record and use for herself.

Fourth session of counselling

Karen is a few minutes late and knocks on my door. No cancellations this time. She's wearing a lovely bright yellow summer dress and looks stunning. Her skin is looking less blotchy and she's wearing more eye makeup. She looks lovely.

K: Sorry I was a little bit late but no cancellations.

C: I know, I'm impressed.

We both laugh.

C: So how would you like to use today?

K: I remembered to bring the photographs and much as I don't want to talk about relationships I think that might be useful. We could start with the photos and get those out of the way.

I nod and Karen brings out an envelope with some prints in. I move the coffee table so she can lay them out for both of us to see.

C: It's important anyway, if we're talking about relationships, to begin with your relationship with yourself so I'm really interested in what photos you chose. Will you tell me a bit about why you chose these?

K: Okay, I'm laying them out chronologically to show me as a baby and our family. There aren't many of us as a family. This one is mum holding me at a few months old.

C: What a beautiful baby you were and your mum looks very young and attractive. I can see you take after her.

K: She loves clothes and always looks good. As the manager of a dress shop she sets an example. I enjoy going shopping with her 'cos she knows exactly what will look good. I think I've learnt that from her.

C: You always look very chic and you wear colours that really suit you. Is this next one you and your brother, Roy?

K: Yes, we don't have many photos of us together. The age gap of ten years was a lot. Once he left home, at about seventeen, he and I didn't see much of each other. He didn't visit home much, which hurt my mum. When he first got together with Becks, I was at university and we kind of got to know each other in a different way. They lived together for a few years and eventually got married when Becks and I were both twenty-three. This one's a photo of the wedding, the only one I have with "the Freak" in it. It was a really good day as long as I kept away from *him*. I'd even thought of not going but I couldn't let Becks and Roy down.

C: Becks looks beautiful and it looks like a happy family occasion.

K: It was good to see mum's family and everyone behaved themselves. This one is of the three of them when Graham was a baby. We used to go out and about even after they had Graham, 'cos mum would babysit. This one is of the four of them just after Emily was born, about eight years ago and this one of all of them with Mum. He hardly ever came to their place.

C: I can see that Roy looks a bit like your father but he has your colouring.

K: They were still happy together then, most of the time. When the economic situation really hit the building trade in London and there was a lot of cheap labour around, he got laid off a couple of times. He'd always been a bit of a drinker but it got much worse. Becks asked him to leave when Emily was about two and he moved back home despite dad being there. Roy spent even more time at the pub as dad was at home all the time, too ill to work. He died five years ago. I didn't go to the funeral.

C: It's hard when these things happen in a family. Your dad learnt to be like that from someone. What's amazing is that most children who are abused, don't go on and abuse other people. Some do and that's very sad for all concerned.

K: It's hard for me to see him as a victim.

C: I'm sure it is Karen and what he did to you was horribly wrong, totally wrong in every way. Do you miss your brother?

K: I see him occasionally, when he's working and sober. I see glimpses of the old fun loving, even protective Roy. He's okay with the kids. He started going out with a new woman a few months ago and that seems to have had a good effect. It'll take something to make him sort himself out. This next one is an up to date photo of Becks and me with the kids.

C: They're really sweet. Graham is very like you and your mum. They're very important to you aren't they?

K: They are. They're both excellent at maths. I help them with homework and talk to them about my job in a fun way. They're both so quick and get stuff about what I do that I'd never have understood at their age. Becks likes me being around but she's protective about not leaving them with me on my own. She knows I'm still using and I respect that. She's nagged me no end about coming off and she's nauseatingly pleased I'm coming here . . . Then there's a photo of me with two friends from Imperial, Paul and Claire taken in our glad rags after our graduation. Claire went on to become a lecturer there and Paul also works in the crazy world of banking. I keep this because it was a really happy time for each of us. They're important to me even though we don't meet up very often. This is one of

Paul and his partner, Jacob. Jacob died of Aids just over a year ago. He battled with it for years. I chose this one of my mum and me, we had a slap up meal in one of Jamie Oliver's restaurants and she asked someone to take this on her phone and then had a print made. Mum and I can chatter together. I like that about her. She doesn't understand much about what I do but I know she's proud of me. We don't talk much about the past but we talk about people we know, clothes, politics going on at work for her and for me, and just stuff. She'd like me to find someone and settle down. She's managed to keep on good terms with Becks and with Roy living at home and she sees the children often. She and Becks' mum are the main babysitters. That's the lot . . . No, I have one more.

Karen looks in the envelope and there is a narrow strip of faded photos which she laid down on the table.

K: This was a Woolworth's photo booth special of my one and only real boyfriend, Billy. He was from Berkeley University on an exchange during our second year at Uni. He was only there for a year and we were friends at first but I loved everything about him. It got a bit serious before he left and then we wrote to each other for about two years but we both moved and lost touch. I had to include this.

C: You look as if you are having fun together. As you look at the photos you've chosen to bring, do you notice anything in particular about you and your family? Also, are there any that are missing that you would have liked to have?

K: Other than my dad, these are all people who are special to me. I suppose I would have liked to have had the kind of life where I would want to have a photo of me and my dad, that relationship has been missing for me, having a real dad.

C: Looking at these photos, there are a lot of real people in your life who love you and who you love.

Karen is thoughtful as she looks again at the photos laid out along the coffee table.

K: That's true, even Roy in his own stupid way, he's been there for me in some ways. I've met some good people. I've been lucky.

C: I notice that there's no photograph of you on your own.

K: I'm not sure I have one of myself on my own.

C: As part the work we're doing is about you building a good relationship with yourself and beginning to trust how much you matter. I wonder if it would be a good idea for you to have a special photograph taken of yourself and keep it on view, especially in view of what you've said about not feeling good about your body. You're the most important support for yourself.

K: That might feel a bit weird but I'll think about it.

C: Good. Is there anything else you'd like to say about the photos?

K: No, it's been interesting.

C: I feel as if I know you better and where you come from. As you say, lots of good connections. That brings us to other connections. Do you want to talk a bit about your relationships and how you felt about your body and yourself as you developed sexually?

K: My sexuality has been fraught with danger, fear, and loss, everything was fucked up by what happened. "The Freak" stole my innocence, my choice to give myself to someone. He destroyed my trust in myself and other people. I felt such a lot of shame about my body for a long time, still do. I protected the outside but always felt I could never wipe myself clean on the inside. No amount of baths or showers could do that . . .

Karen clenches her fists and her jaw as she speaks.

K: After I was raped by *him* I felt that no-one would ever touch me again. I actually think that if anyone had tried, I'd have killed them. There was a raw rage bunched up inside me and once I did hit out at a guy in a club who pushed himself hard up against me on the dance floor and pinched my bottom. I bloodied his nose and it was only because Becks and Roy held me off him that I stopped. I saw red and I can't even remember but they told me I wouldn't stop screaming until they took me outside and Roy slapped my face. I was scared to get close to anyone, scared what they might do, and scared of what I might do. Even when I was high on drugs I was usually with a group of people that I trusted. I kept myself away from any kind of sexual contact. I became good at camouflage, avoidance, disappearing at the right time. I think when I was at senior school my sexual feelings turned into anger and I used that to compete, especially with the boys. I was way ahead of any of them at maths, computing, all of the sciences. I made their world my world. I relentless pursued the perfection of numbers, facts, technology. I trusted numbers not to let me down. For years, the only person who ever got through the walls I built around those kinds of feelings was Billy. He was different, sounded like a character in a Hollywood movie, and he was a really nice guy. He never pushed me. We liked each other. I felt like I'd known him before. We became friends. He knew that I hid away, knew I'd been hurt but never asked about it and he respected me. We were both geeks on the computer. He'd been hurt in his life by an older brother and it's like he understood. We messed around like kids. We'd play fight but he sensed just how far he could go and he'd stop. We'd both read and do stuff on the computer with our legs up the wall. He gave me some of my childhood back. He never came on to me and yet there grew up a powerful chemistry between us. The inevitable time came when his time was up and he had to go back. Perhaps, I let myself feel what I did because I knew he was going away. I chose to have sex properly for the first time with him. I like to think of that as my first time.

C: What a healing relationship that sounds, for both of you.

K: I think we certainly went some way towards healing each other. I missed him like crazy. We wrote for a year or two and then the letters got less frequent and we both moved a couple of times. I do wonder sometimes what happened to him. He was a very special person to me.

C: Any other long term relationships since then?

K: I went through a very promiscuous stage when I was first taking cocaine and partying a lot. Honestly, I can hardly remember any of them. It's a bit of a haze. I got several lectures from Becks and Claire. I didn't dare tell Paul because of the Aids thing. I was very lucky to get out of that destructive behaviour, relatively unscathed. Getting my flat was very important for me. I didn't want anyone there who I couldn't trust. It had to be my safe place. So, since having this job, my main relationship has been to work. I get such a buzz from it and it takes a lot of my time. I honestly haven't met anyone I wanted to have a relationship with. I've dated a few friends of people I know, several blind dates, even had a brief fling with internet dating but I found it impossible to trust anyone so it never got past coffee at lunch time. That's where I've got to.

C: How do you feel about that?

K: Sometimes I imagine the sort of guy I'd like to be with but I've got used to being on my own . . . not sure I want anyone in my life. I don't think I'm afraid, just switched off somehow.

C: What happens when you meet someone you might be interested in?

K: I suppose I put up the defences. I go into professional mode and distance myself a bit. I can see myself doing it. It all feels too much like hard work. I'm tired enough as I am, the idea of having to work at a relationship as well . . . The idea of explaining what's happened to me and why I'm the way I am . . . having to explain the cocaine . . . I don't know, it just seems much easier to stay single.

C: Do you feel you're missing out on something you'd like to have in your life?

K: When I see other people with their partners, even Roy with his new woman. Becks has a longish term, "friend"; Claire is married to a lovely man and is talking about children; Paul is settled with a great guy who helped him through the death of his partner. Yes, sometimes I feel like the only single person in the world when I go to some function or other.

C: Well, yet again, the most important person for you to build a good relationship with right now is yourself?

K: It's what they say, whoever "they" are. Love yourself before you can love someone else.

C: Well maybe it's possible to do both at once.

We both laugh.

C: How do you feel about having children?

K: Occasionally, when I leave Graham and Emily, I get a real pang and longing for my own children. That feeling passes. I do worry that I would lose my cool with any children of my own. I think, again, I'm scared of what I could do to them . . . scared I could be like *him*. What if I was like my mother and didn't see if they were being abused by a partner. I couldn't bring children into the world who could be hurt like that.

C: Realistically, do you honestly think you would be the sort of person, not to notice?

Karen grins at me.

K: No, at work and socially, I pick up any hint or innuendo about anything from 100 metres away.

We both laugh.

C: As for that potential for anger. Do you still lose control as you did when you were a teenager?

K: No, I don't but I do have to work very hard when I see children being hurt to keep that down.

C: There's a huge difference between having the feeling and doing something about it.

K: That's true. I'm not sure that I do trust myself.

C: Then maybe that's something you can work on if you pursue longer term counselling. Did you manage to contact anyone?

K: Yes, I phoned Mary Chase, the person you told me about. I've fixed up an appointment for early next week, before we meet. I thought about your suggestion and it seemed like a good idea to meet with her before we end. I got to speak to her on the phone and told her that we'd been working together and she thought it was a good idea for her and me to meet before this ends. She sounded nice and sent you her regards. She's starting a new evening group in about two months and could have a place for me there, depending how it all goes.

C: That sounds fantastic. You've done so well. How do you feel about moving on to working with someone else?

K: I've gone from seeing counselling as something that can't help to seeing that it can be practical, supportive, and really effective. You do kind of make me do the work anyway.

Karen looks at me a bit sheepishly and grins.

C: Yes, I guess I do. Did you re-organise the medical tests at your GP and get the results back?

K: Yes, I finally got to the hospital and they should be back in the next few days. I'll go in for a chat with her. I've carried on with the acupuncture which seems to be helping a bit. I'm not sure I would have been able to cope with last week otherwise. I get what you were saying before about everything I do that's positive, like the bricks, together they're helping me make it through this. I feel stronger, I really do. I even had a go at some of the breathing exercises. In fact, I had a bit of a row with someone at work and I couldn't calm myself, no matter what I did. There was no way I could think of sitting still but I took myself off to a café nearby and pretended to read the paper but was actually doing a visualisation. I couldn't believe it but it did calm me down a bit. So I used it a couple of times, once on the tube.

C: Again, you're building up a tool bag with skills and support that you can choose to use or not. How have you got on focusing on the choices you make?

K: In noticing the smaller choices, I've become more aware of the bigger choices, even that I have a choice at all. I think the drugs have numbed out so much of my awareness and maybe that's been the point of them,

I've been in automatic pilot a lot of the time. Bringing choices into focus kind of brings me into focus more. It's hard work because it's more decisions I have to make and I make too many at work already. In a weird way, it feels as if I'm waking up from a deep sleep, do you know what I mean?

C: I think I do. It seems easier sometimes to go along with what other people want to give you, but to *stop* for even the smallest moment to consider what you *really* want is empowering. Also, to choose to do something *different* is a bit of an adventure, it can be fun.

K: Yeah. It throws me back on myself and sometimes I come up with new ideas. That's creative isn't it?

C: I think it is and I think that's possibly one of the biggest aspects of the self that gets blotted out by drink, drugs, being preoccupied with people, work, whatever.

K: Maybe that's the difference between living and existing?

C: Could well be.

K: I know it's nearly time to end but sometimes the things we talk about here, just blow my mind and I go away thinking about things I've not thought about before.

C: One of the things I enjoy so much about working with you Karen is how bright you are, and how you question, and like Graham and Emily, how quickly you take up quite difficult ideas and run with them.

K: Thank you and ditto, I enjoy talking with you and I feel a real acceptance. You've never told me off for swearing, it drives my boss mad at work.

C: Personally, I think that some swear words are just fantastically expressive. So, one more session next week. How does that feel?

K: I can't say I not scared of working with someone else and the thought of a group is absolutely terrifying but I was scared when I came here and it's been amazing so . . . I'm up for anything that will help get this done.

C: What resources within yourself can you draw upon that would give you more confidence?

K: I face new situations all day at work, but this is different . . . I suppose I won't do the group straight away and I can choose not to do it until I'm really ready . . . I can remember how it was coming here and that I've been able to do it . . . I could put your name in my pocket.

We both laugh

C: That sounds a great idea . . . Anything else?

K: Well, I think it will help to know everyone in the group will know what it's like, we're all in the same boat . . . I'd forgotten that. They'll be scared too, especially if it's a new group. We're all going to be there for each other, I hope, and if it doesn't work for me, I can leave the group and carry on with the individual work and other things I find helpful . . . I suppose I get stuck sometimes thinking that I have to go through with things that I don't want to do, but I have a choice . . . I have a choice.

C: That sounds really good. Let's find a time for next week.

We make an appointment and I watch for a moment to see Karen walk down the corridor, she seems taller.

Final session of counselling

I collected Karen from the waiting room and we both remarked on the fact that there were no longer any apologies for cancellations needed. Karen looked stunning in a beautiful teal and turquoise long-sleeved summer dress. She sat comfortably back in her seat crossing her legs.

C: You've done it Karen, three weeks running; that's a real commitment to yourself. How do you feel about that?

K: I could find something I've messed up about but instead I'm *choosing* to feel a little smug.

We both laughed.

C: How do you feel about it being the last session?

K: A bit scared. In a weird way I feel as if the beginning and the decision to commit to my recovery from the drugs and the past has been completed and achieved. I know it means more of the same, a bloody hard grind at that, but it'll be different because I think part of me has stopping fighting myself, if that makes sense.

C: It does. I have a suggestion of something you could do today to round this work off but I'd like to hear from you first about anything you'd like to do or talk about. It'd be good to save some time for us to review our work together; over to you first.

K: I went to see Mary on Monday and together we've put together a programme of treatment, which is pretty adaptable. What we've covered here all seems to fit in with how she works as well. I'll carry on doing the acupuncture. I'll have another full medical check at the Rehab. Centre and they'll liaise with my own doctor. I may decide to join the support group that Mary runs but I don't have to sign up for that just yet. I've signed up for a yoga class there which includes about twenty minutes meditation and breathing exercises. They even have their own gym which I can use as part of the whole package. I've yet to think about how I'm going to find time for all this, on the other hand knowing that work will get messed up anyway if I don't find the time makes it easier to commit. Living is important too, that's what this has been all about really hasn't it?

C: I think it has. You've managed to find the time to come here. You won't have to spend excess energy on doing everything perfectly and being so "on your case" because of the effects of the cocaine.

K: True . . . I do feel differently about it all. I can have reflexology and massage although I like going to this friend of Becks. Who knows, I may do both. I feel a little odd about having a massage, feet is fine, whole body, not yet.

C: It's understandable considering that your body boundaries have been so abused. You could ask for an Indian Head Massage or just neck and shoulders to begin with and see how that feels.

K: I quite fancy a head massage, sometimes my head feels as if I'm wearing one of those torture type helmets that they used to tighten until I suppose it kills you.

C: That sounds horrible. I'm glad you sound so positive about doing this for yourself and you know you don't have to do it all at once. Did you get your blood test results from the doctor?

K: Yes, I phoned in and I do need to see her. I couldn't get an appointment to see her this week and I didn't want to see the locum. I've booked in to see her after the weekend. The rehab doctor uses both homeopathic treatment and conventional drugs. I know my doctor is open to that kind of thing as long as I check in with her regularly. She doesn't want me to disappear, which I can understand. See, I had a similar conversation with her.

C: I'm glad to hear that you have good medical support and it sounds as if it could all work together well. Anything else you'd like to use today for?

K: Just to say I was going to drop down to one gram a day after last time and I thought about the change over from seeing you to the Rehab and rather than just acting, as I would normally and force myself to do it, I chose to wait until I get settled in the new programme. I made a choice that I really thought about. I haven't taken more than I've agreed with myself and I've handled the cravings, which get really bad some times, by doing lots of "brick" things. I'm not under any illusion about this process. I spoke with Mary about that too. I know it's going to continue to be bloody hard for quite a while.

C: When you're used to doing things quickly and cocaine speeds everything up in a false way, it can be the hardest thing to accept the necessity of doing something gradually and taking your time. I know you're committed to coming off the drugs. You don't have to prove that. When we spoke at the end of last time, I thought about all the things you've put in place in a matter of weeks. What you came here to do was to begin a process and find a reason for commitment to yourself. You've certainly done that. Perhaps you could to add that to your poster.

K: I will. I'm keen to know what you've got in store for me this week.

We both smiled.

C: It's just a suggestion based on what you were saying about relationships last week. I was thinking about your eight-year-old feeling vulnerable in relationships for obvious reasons and maybe your ten-year-old feeling afraid of what she might be capable of. What you did to your father was very brave and in other circumstances might be wrong or illegal but you were protecting yourself and I'm aware that you had seen your brother be violent to your dad to protect himself. My suggestion is that we give some time to a role play between you and both the eight-year-old and the ten-year-old. This would involve using the two empty chairs here and you moving between the three chairs to do the role play. The aim is to build a connection between the three of you which will carry you forward through this difficult time of change and recovery and may help you to break through those old attachments to feeling vulnerable and afraid of yourself in relationships. What do you think?

K: When you say that you have a suggestion, I feel a mixture of fear and excitement. I get what you're saying and I'm okay about having a go. No idea if I can do it but that's how I've felt about everything we've done here and it's been okay. Let's do it.

C: I think first, as you've already done some work with the eight-year-old, there needs to be some levelling up so that you equally build a connection with your ten-year-old. I'd suggest a short exercise with her first. Are you alright with that?

K: Yeah.

There is a small cushion on each of the empty chairs in the room so I pick one up and give it to Karen.

> *C*: Okay, I want you to place this cushion on your lap and imagine that this is ten-year-old Karen. Could you tell me what she would be dressed in?

> *K*: She'd have a denim skirt, a bright red long-sleeved T-shirt and a fine knitted denim-blue cardigan, red socks, and blue trainers.

> *C*: How would she have her hair?

> *K*: A pony tail with red slides on either side.

> *C*: I'd like you to close your eyes and really feel her sitting on your lap.

Karen shuts her eyes and takes a few moments.

> *C*: Then imagine that you shrink her to about a centimetre high and find that pool of love that you have inside you where you feel love for Graham and Emily . . . Invite her into that place of love to stay with you . . . Imagine making a commitment to: protect her; take care of her; listen to her; love her . . . Allow yourself to feel what that's like for you and for her. Take some time for this . . . When you feel there is a real connection between you, come back into the room and notice a colour and shape to ground you back here.

During this exercise Karen picks up the cushion and is holding it tight. She is still and takes quite a few minutes before she opens her eyes. She looks softer.

> *K*: At first, she felt quite rigid, I really hugged her and then it was easier to find that place in myself for her and for her to trust it. You were right. I felt very protective of the eight-year-old but because of what I did to *him* I didn't even really see my ten-year-old as a child anymore.

Karen's eyes filled with tears and we sat in silence for a few moments.

> *C*: A ten-year-old is very much a child, still at junior school; you shouldn't have had to experience what you did. But, bad things happen to children all over the world, it's a part of life. It's important to normalise that too; not accept it but normalise it . . . it happens. There are many kinds of abuse: physical, psychological, sexual, children being overworked, and forced into early marriages. What I know is that children can recover from these things.

K: I'm aware of being sad when I see children starving, beaten, hurt. It's a part of our world. I found it hard being at university around young people who were able to be quite naïve about *life*, I felt a strong sense of loss of my . . . innocence . . . of my . . . childhood. On the other hand, I know it gave me strengths they didn't have. It made me hungry to be successful. This has helped 'cos I think I felt weird about what I did, as if there was something wrong with me, but I'm glad I'm not a push over either . . . when I went the other way and got into one night stands . . . I think I was trying to prove no-one could get to me . . . I was being like the guys, but the person who hurt me most was myself. It was hell and I ended up hating myself. I learnt that I could stop doing that . . . it's the same now . . . I need to know I can stop taking drugs. I can see it's what I need to do for myself so I can move on from all of this past stuff.

C: You can never get back your innocence and childhood and maybe that will be something you need to grieve for, but, you can get back that sense of joy and playfulness and learn to balance that with work. It sounds as if you enjoy being with your niece and nephew.

K: They're great fun and help me to forget work and everything else.

C: Are you up for doing this role play with your own eight- and ten-year-old?

K: Yeah.

C: Choose who you are going to put where and place the chairs where you'd like them to be, maybe a bit closer to you.

Karen pulls the chairs towards her and turns her own chair a little to face them.

C: What would be the best focus in terms of what you want to achieve from talking to your eight- and ten-year-old?

K: I feel that my eight-year-old feels too scared and vulnerable to risk being intimate with someone and I've been afraid of what my ten-year-old might do . . . she feels more unpredictable.

C: So you could ask each of them what they need from you and even ask if they need anything from each other to feel safe.

K: Yeah that sounds okay.

C: What is each of them wearing.

K: Eight-year-old Karen is in this chair nearest to me and she is wearing dark green trousers, and a bright green T-shirt, with bright green canvas shoes. Her hair is shoulder length and loose. Ten-year-old Karen is wearing the same as before, red and blue denim.

C: Can you take a few moments and really imagine them here with us. The idea is then that you ask them a question and then you go and sit in their chair and imagine that you become the eight- and ten-year-old, and speak as them.

K: That's okay.

C: They're all yours.

Karen takes a few moments to close her eyes and then looks at each chair in turn.

K: I need to talk to both of you. I want to help you trust that I can help keep me . . . us safe so that we can maybe get to know someone really well without getting hurt or hurting them. I'll start with you as the youngest little Karen. What do you need from me to be less scared about me getting close to someone, like I did with Billy?

Karen looks over at me and gets up and sits in the eight-year-old empty chair. She sits right back in the chair and shuts her eyes.

K-eight: . . . I need time . . . to trust someone. You've hurried into relationships before I'm ready. You didn't do that with Billy and that was okay . . . since then you've made it scary.

Karen goes back to her chair.

K: That's helpful. I've got too used to rushing into things not thinking of protecting us. What made it possible with Billy was that we made friends first. Thank you. If I make friends with someone first, would that be easier for you?

Karen goes back to sit in the eight-year-old chair.

K-eight: Yes. I'm only just beginning to trust you . . . how can I trust someone else I don't know?

Karen goes back to her own chair.

K: It's good that you're beginning to trust me. I've not given you much reason to. I get that you need more time. If I did this kind of thing at home and asked if you felt safe with someone, would you tell me if you felt safe enough?

Karen swops chairs again.

K-eight: I'd like that.

Karen swops back to her own chair.

K: Is there anything else you'd like from me to feel safe?

Karen swops over again.

K-eight: Only to stop going away.

Karen swops again.

K: I think I know what you mean and I'm working on that as hard as I can. Thank you. I want to talk to my ten-year-old now and then I'll talk to you again.

Karen turns towards the ten-year-old chair.

K: What about you. Is there anything you need from me to feel safe from me, from yourself, or from other people?

Karen moves into the other chair and sits on the edge of the seat.

K-ten: I don't want to feel odd any more . . . don't want to be out of control. I need to know that you and me can say no and I agree with her, do things more slow.

She nods towards the other empty chair and Karen goes back to her own chair to answer.

K: You're both saying the same thing. If I can take charge of my life and keep myself safe, you'll both feel safe?

Karen looks at both chairs and then swops back to the ten-year-old chair.

K-ten: If I feel safe, she'll feel safe and then I can stop looking after her for you.

Karen goes back to her chair.

K: Is that how you felt that you had to look after her?

Karen swops over to her chair

K-ten: Of course, who else was going to?

Karen goes back to her chair to answer.

K: Okay, I get this. I've really let you down and put a lot on you. I'm so sorry. I didn't know this. I promise I'll look after both of you the best I can. Do either of you have anything else you want to say to me?

Karen goes over to the ten-year-old chair first.

> *K-ten*: I need you to stop disappearing as well. I don't need you to be here all the time but I need you to listen to me when I'm scared, to think about what makes me scared, and what makes me most scared is when I feel forced into something that is too much for me and then I get so I just want to hit out at someone.

Karen goes back to her own chair

> *K*: I get what you're saying. I put myself and you under terrible pressure sometimes and I need to think ahead. I need to make space in my head . . . to find some peace. I can do this and you've both given me a reason to. Thank you. Do you have anything else to say?

Karen goes back to the ten-year-old chair.

> *K-ten*: Not today.

Karen goes back to her own chair and addresses the same question to the eight-year-old.

> *K*: Do you have anything else to say?

Karen goes back to the eight-year-old chair.

> *K-eight*: Only that I like playing with Emily and Graham . . . and you.

Karen goes back to her own chair.

> *K*: Thank you . . . both of you. I think you've taught me that I need to be aware of taking care of all of myself.

Karen looked over at me.

> *K*: Well that was weird but felt very real.

> *C*: Shall we put the chairs back in their places?

We move one chair each and sit down again.

> *C*: How do you feel now?

> *K*: A bit humble really . . . I thought it was all about taking care of the externals, work, home, finances, clothes, even body but there is this whole world inside of memories, experiences, feelings, beliefs, expectations . . . I'm just beginning to get to know parts of me I've not even thought about.

> *C*: You've begun to open yourself and all along you were afraid of that "can of worms" but there are so many resources within yourself including

these lovely two parts of you that in their own way have worked hard to keep you safe.

K: Yes. It's weird that I've been blocking out the good bits from the past as well as the bad. I need them as much as they need me . . . maybe they're what will keep me on track and committed. I strangely feel quite excited even though it's a little daunting.

C: Has this been an okay way to end our sessions together?

K: Weird as usual but yes, I feel . . . softer . . . tearful . . . I'm sad that we're ending but I'm really grateful for . . . so much really. I'm glad I came and I had no idea what I'd find but whatever it is, I know I want more of it.

C: I've enjoyed working with you and I'm glad you did commit to yourself and come to these last three sessions. I know you'll do this. You already are. You're a very bright and resourceful young woman and I've watched you develop a lot in a very short time. I believe you are completely ready to do this and I wish you luck with your recovery.

K: I really want to do this and I believe I will this time. You've shown me that support is not "giving up"; it's a real strength to ask for help. I felt so stuck when I came and I know you've made me do the work but you've given me real support and shown me simple things I can do to help myself. Thank you.

Karen reaches down into her bag, placed beside her chair and pulls out an envelope.

K: I wanted to give you this 'cos I knew you'd appreciate it.

I open the white envelope and there is a card with a beautiful sunflower on it. Inside is a thank you on one side and stuck on the other side is a lovely photo of Karen in her lovely teal and turquoise dress that she is wearing today.

K: You said there was no photo of me on my own so I thought you'd appreciate having one and I did one for myself as well. I went to a proper photographer to have it taken.

C: I can see that, it is absolutely lovely and means a lot to me. You bring with you such a beautiful energy Karen. I know you will make your own life and future, just the way you choose. It really has been a pleasure to work with you. Thank you for this.

We both get up and Karen asks me for a hug on the way out, which I give her. She is a little tearful, well actually we both are.

References

Cyrulnik, B. (2009). *Resilience: How to Gain Strength from Childhood Adversity*. London: Penguin.

Harris, T. A. (2012). *I'm Ok, You're Ok*. London: Cornerstone.

Liedloff, J. (1989). *The Continuum Concept*. London: Arkana.

Yudkin, J. (2012). *Pure White and Deadly: How Sugar is Killing Us and What We Can Do to Stop It*. London: Viking Adult.

Useful books, articles, and websites

The author has a useful counselling website/blog which contains various counselling tools and a series of relaxation exercises. This is accessed on: counsellingcasestories.wordpress.com

Addiction

Books

Bower, M., Hale, R., & Wood, H. (Eds.) (2013). *Addictive States of Mind*. London: Karnac.

Bryant-Jeffries, R. (2006). An addicted society? *Therapy Today, 17*(2): 4–5.

Ford, C., Oliver, J., & Whitehead, B. (2006). Treating drug users: a collaborative method. *Therapy Today, 17*(2):17–20.

Liedloff, J. (1989). *The Continuum Concept*. London: Arkana.

Schaverien, J. (2004). Boarding school: the trauma of the "privileged" child. *Journal of Analytical Psychology, 49*(5): 683–705.

Sinclair, M. (2010). *Fear and Self-Loathing in the City, a Guide to Staying Sane in the Square Mile*. London: Karnac.

Wilders S., & Robinson, S. (2006). Addiction: is counselling sufficient? *Therapy Today, 17*(2):11–15.

Yudkin, J. (2012). *Pure White and Deadly: How Sugar is Killing Us and What We Can Do to Stop It*. London: Viking Adult.

Websites

(all sites last accessed on 30 July 2013)
www.actionaddiction.org.uk
www.drugabuse.gov
www.drugscope.org.uk
www.helpguide.org/topics/addiction.htm
www.nhs.uk/livewell/addiction
www.talktofrank.com

Anorexia

Books

Alexander, J., &Treasure, J. (Eds.) (2011). *A Collaborative Approach to Eating Disorders*. London: Routledge.

Bordo, S. (2003). *Unbearable Weight: Feminism, Western Culture and the Body*. London: University of California Press.

Brown, K. (2009). Emotional eating. *Therapy Today*, 20(6):16–19.

Buckroyd, J. (2008). Eating disorders and disordered eating: underlying emotional issues. *AUCC Journal*, May: 2–5.

Corstorphine, E. (2008). Addressing emotions in the eating disorders: schema mode work. In: J. Buckroyd & S. Rother (Eds.), *Psychological Responses to Eating Disorders and Obesity Recent and Innovative Work* (pp. 85–100). Chichester: Wiley and Sons.

Crisp, A. H., Joughin, N. J., Halek, C., & Bowyer, C. (1996) *Anorexia Nervosa: The Wish to Change*. East Sussex: Psychology Press.

Davies, P. (2004). Eating disorders prevention and management. *AUCC Journal, Spring*: 6–9.

Deacon, L. (2008). My body my rights. *Therapy Today*, 19(5): 32–34.

Fairburn, C. (1995). *Overcoming Binge Eating*. New York: Guildford Press.

Hayman, P. (2008). Challenging and changing eating disorders. *AUCC Journal*, May: 6–9.

King, M. B., & Bhugra, D. (1989). Eating disorders: lessons from a cross-cultural study. *Psychological Medicine*, 19(4): 955–958.

Lask, B., & Bryant-Waugh, R. (Eds.) (2012). *Eating Disorders in Childhood and Adolescence*. New York: Routledge.

Nardone, G., Milanese, R., & Verbitz, T. (2005). *Prison of Food, Research and Treatment of Eating Disorder*. London: Karnac.

Orbach, S. (2005). *Hunger Strike, The Anorexic's Struggle as a Metaphor for our Age*. London: Karnac.

Websites

(all sites last accessed on 30 July 2013)
www.b-eat.co.uk
www.eating-disorders.org.uk
www.nationaleating disorders.org
www.nhs.uk/conditions/eating-disorders

Boarding schools

Books

Duffell, N. (2011). Old school ties. *Therapy Today*, 22(3): 10–15.
Duffell, N., & Bland R. (2000). *The Making of Them: The British Attitude to Children and the Boarding School System*. London: Lone Arrow.
Le Carre, J. (1995). *Our Game*. London: Hodder & Stoughton.
Ogden, T. (1992). *The Primitive Edge of Experience*. London: Karnac.
Schaverien, J. (2004). Boarding school: the trauma of the "privileged" child. *Journal of Analytical Psychology*, 49(5): 683–705.
Schaverien, J. (2011). Boarding school syndrome: broken attachments a hidden trauma. *British Journal of Psychotherapy*, 27(2): 138–155.
Schaverien, J. (2011). Lost for words. *Therapy Today*, 22(3): 18–21.

Websites

(all sites last accessed on 30 July 2013)
www.boardingrecovery.com/images/survivingtheprivilege.pdf
www.boardingschoolsurvivors.co.uk
www.relatenow.co.uk/content/relationship-counselling-boarding-school-survivors
www.wellaware.org.uk10119-association-for-boarding-school-survivors

Depression

Books

Biorgvinsson, T., & Rozqvist, J. (2008). *Cognitive-Behavioural Therapy for Depression: A Practical Guide to Management and Treatment*. London: Routledge.
Flemons, D., & Gralnik, L. M. (2013). *Relational Suicide Assessment: Risks, Resources, and Possibilities for Safety*. New York: Norton.

Harris, D. L. (Ed.) (2010). *Counting Our Losses*. New York: Routledge.

Henden, J. (2008). *Preventing Suicide: The Solution Focused Approach.* London: Wiley & Sons.

Pope, A. (2013). The depths of depression. *Therapy Today, 24*(6): 26–29.

Rowe, D. (2003). *Depression: The Way out of Your Prison* (3rd edn). London: Routledge.

Silver, R. (2007). *The Silver Drawing Test and Draw a Story: Assessing Depression, Aggression, and Cognitive Skills.* New York: Routledge.

Tugendhat, J. (2005). *Living with Grief and Loss*. London: Sheldon Press.

Williams, M., Segal, Z. V., Teasdale, J., & Kabat-Zinn, J. (Eds.) (2007). *The Mindful Way Through Depression: Freeing Yourself from Chronic Unhappiness.* New York: Guilford Press.

Websites

(all sites last accessed on 30 July 2013)
www.depressionalliance.org
www.mind.org.uk
www.nhs.uk/conditions/depression/pages/introduction.aspx
www.nimh.nih.gov/health/topics/depression

Multicultural issues

Books

Bodhakari (2008). The Prison of the Self. *Therapy Today, 19*(6): 30–33.

Brazier, C. (2003). *Buddhist Psychology*. London: Robinson.

Chunt, A. (2007). Daring to be different. *Therapy Today, 18*(4): 31–34.

Davey, G., & Zhao, X. (2012). Counselling in China. *Therapy Today, 23*(9): 13–17.

Ellis, B. (2004). Racial politics and therapy. *Counselling and Psychotherapy Journal, 15*(8): 40–41.

Imberti, P. (2008). The immigrant's odyssey. *Therapy Today, 19*(6): 2–9.

Kapadia, M. (2008). Adapting to difference: the hairdryer theory, working with clients from non-Western cultures. *Therapy Today, 19*(6): 16–20.

Lago, C. (2006). *Race, Culture and Counselling: The Ongoing Challenge* (2nd edn). Oxford: Oxford University Press.

Laungani, P. (2004). *Asian Perspectives in Counselling and Psychotherapy.* East Sussex: Brunner-Routledge.

McKenzie-Mavinga, I. (2009). *Black Issues in the Therapeutic Process*. London: Palgrave-Macmillan.

Pointon, C. (2004). Does our training embrace difference and diversity? *Counselling and Psychotherapy Journal*, 15(8): 5.

Selin, H., & Davey, G. (2012). *Happiness Across Cultures: Views of Happiness and Quality of Life in Non-Western Cultures*. New York: Springer.

Websites

(all sites last accessed on 30 July 2013)
www.asianfamilycounselling.org.uk
www.asianwomencentre.org.uk
www.baatn.org.uk
www.ciac.co.uk
www.eugenebaatn.wordpress.com
www.mapesburyclinic.org.uk
www.myh.org.uk
www.nafsiyat.org.uk
www.southallblacksisters.org.uk
www.ubuntucommunityservices.org.uk/index.php/counselling

Relationship counselling

Books

Baron-Cohen, S. (2007). *The Essential Difference: Men, Women and the Extreme Male Brain*. London: AllenLane/Penguin Press.

Cameron, D. (2006). *The Myth of Mars and Venus*. Oxford: Oxford University Press.

Clulow, C. (2007). Attachment, couples and the talking cure. *Therapy Today*, 18(6): 4–6.

Fisher, H. (2004). *Why We Love: The Nature and Chemistry of Romantic Love*. New York: Henry Holt.

Harris, T. A. (2012). *I'm Ok, You're Ok*. London: Cornerstone.

Johnson, S. (2007). Emotion in couple therapy. *Therapy Today*, 18(6): 7–11.

Mutanda, A. (2013). *How to do Relationships: A Step-by-step Guide to Nurturing Your Relationship and Making Love Last*. London: Relate/Vermilion.

Websites

(all sites last accessed on 30 July 2013)
www.arc-relationshipcounselling.co.uk
www.marriagecare.org.uk
www.nhs.uk/livewell/counselling/Pages/Couplestherapyrealstory.aspx
www.relate.org.uk
www.relatenow.co.uk/content/relationship-counselling-boarding-school-
   survivors
www.relationships-scotlandccs.org.uk

Sexual abuse and trauma

Books

Claire, B., Draucker, C. B., Martsolf, D. S. (2006). *Counselling Survivors of Childhood Sexual Abuse* (3rd edn). London: Sage.

Cyrulnik, B. (2009). *Resilience: How to Gain Strength from Childhood Adversity*. London: Penguin.

Fromm, G. M. (2012). *Lost in Transmission: Studies of Trauma Across Generations*. London: Karnac.

McKinnon, M. (2008). *Repair Your Life: A Programme for Recovery from Incest and Childhood Sexual Abuse*. Google eBook.

Mitchell, R. (2007). Fix you? *Therapy Today, 18*(6): 12–14.

Sanderson, C. (2006). *Counselling Adult Survivors of Child Sexual Abuse*. London: Jessica Kingsley.

Walker, M. (2003). *Abuse: Questions and Answers for Counsellors and Therapists*. London: Wiley-Blackwell.

Websites

(all sites last accessed on 30 July 2013)
www.havoca.org/HAVOCA_home.htm
www.napac.org.uk
www.nspcc.org.uk
www.stopitnow.org.uk
www.victimsupport.org.uk

INDEX

15